Twelve Mormon Homes

Visited in Succession on a Journey through Utah to Arizona

By Elizabeth Wood Kane

Published by Pantianos Classics

ISBN-13: 978-1-78987-529-4

First published in 1874

Contents

Pandemonium or Arcadia: Which? 4
Payson 12
Nephi 17
Chicken Creek - The Sevier 32
Scipio 35
Cedar Springs - Fillmore 39
Cove Creek Fort 44
Prairie Dog Hollow - Indian Creek 50
Beaver 56
Buckhorn Spring - Red Creek 59
Parowan 62
Parowan to Cedar 66
Kannarra 71
Southern Ram of the Basin 77
Bellevue 79
To St. George 82

Pandemonium or Arcadia: Which?

"As I walked through the wilderness of this world, I lighted on a certain place where was a den."

- The Pilgrim's Progress

Brigham Young, "President of the Church of Jesus Christ of Latter-Day Saints," makes an annual journey of inspection south, visiting the settlements of his people from the Great Salt Lake to the Arizona border.

My husband was invited to join his party last winter, and I accompanied him with my two children, boys of eight and ten.

We left Salt Lake City early one December morning, while the stars were still shining in the frosty dawn. At the depot a crowd of Mormons were assembled to see their leader off, and a committee of them filled the special car, on the Utah Southern Railroad, in which we made the first stage of our journey. We ran down Salt Lake Valley while the mountains on our left were still in shadow, but the golden sunrise was resting on the tops of those on our right, and gradually slanting down towards the plain. The snow had melted from all but the highest summits, and some of these were only veined with it in their ravines.

Stepping to the rear of the car to look at a trestle-work that was very long and very high for timberless Utah, we had a beautiful view of the city we had left, nestling at the foot of the mountain; the blue Salt Lake, and Antelope Island in the distance. The dreamy tranquillity of the scene was succeeded by a busy one at Sandy Station. We stopped to visit the newly-established smelting works of an English company, managed by Germans. Outside, lay heaps of ore, stacks of ingots of silver, and pigs of lead. Entering, we found ourselves just in time to see a stream of boiling metal run from one caldron to another. It looked transparent, having a black clearness like alcohol, and as I stood looking down into it I could scarcely believe that it was lead. The works had only been in operation a fortnight, but the foreman was in great delight over the results obtained by a new process, for the patent-right of which, he said, his company had paid $100,000.

"It is as pure as the Swansea Works, and purer than we can obtain it in Germany," he exclaimed. "Only two pennyweights of silver to the ton of lead!" To my ignorance it seemed that the more silver there was, the better; but I found that he meant to express the complete separation of the metals effected by the new process. He wished to prove this on the spot by an interesting test, but our engine was hooting its impatience, and we were forced to resume our seats in the train. Mine was beside a sweet-looking elderly lady who, with her widowed sister, was to leave us at the next station to attend the meeting of a Female Relief Society. She introduced the subject of polygamy abruptly, telling me, among other things, that to her it had been long known as revelation, [1] "Brother Joseph" having revealed it to her thirty-six years ago. She had proved its wisdom since! I learned that this woman had been one of Smith's own wives; the first "plural wife" of the sect! Since his death she had espoused another saintly personage.

A few minutes' ride from Sandy Station brought us opposite the gorge of the "Little Cottonwood," It was hard to realize that thousands of men were busy in the recesses of that wild and desolate-looking ravine. Yet the famous, or *in*famous, Emma Mine is there; and opposite, across the sunny Jordan Valley, some twelve or fifteen miles off — though seeming scarcely three miles distant in the clear atmosphere — we saw Bingham Canon, another noted mining locality. A little distance down the line, clouds of smoke were pouring from the tall chimneys of another smelting establishment.

So far we were still in "Gentile" country. The Mormon president discourages mining among his people, but I suspect that a great many of his richer followers are interested in mining speculations.

We left the train at Lehi. It was not an attractive-looking place, and I went no farther than the depot, where a crowd of stages, baggage wagons, and hurrying men intercepted the view. As I sat warming myself at the ticket-office stove, a young lady, chief telegrapher from the Salt Lake office, with her dress neatly looped over her balmoral skirt, tripped up to the table where sat the Lehi telegraph clerk, a woman, too; and, after an effusive greeting, the pair subsided into business. The Lehi office was thoroughly inspected; satisfactorily, as it appeared from the tones of both ladies; the curt, dry, question and answer of the catechism ending in a pleasant chat, seasoned with adjectives and girlish interjections. It was an example of one of the contradictions of Mormonism. Thousands of years behind us in some of their customs; in others, you would think these people the most forward children of the age. They close no career on a woman in Utah by which she can earn a living.

I strolled out on the platform afterwards, to find President Young preparing for our journey — as he did every morning afterwards — by a personal inspection of the condition of every wheel, axle, horse and mule, and suit of harness belonging to the party. He was peering like a well-intentioned wizard into every nook and cranny, pointing out a defect here and there with his odd, six-sided staff engraved with the hieroglyphs of many measures; more useful, though less romantic, than a Runic wand. He wore a great surtout, reaching almost to his feet, of dark-green cloth (Mahomet color?) lined with fur, a fur collar, cap, and pair of sealskin boots with the undyed fur outward. I was amused at his odd appearance; but as he turned to address me, he removed a hideous pair of green goggles, and his keen, blue-gray eyes met mine with their characteristic look of shrewd and cunning insight. I felt no further inclination to laugh. His photographs, accurate enough in other respects, altogether fail to give the expression of his eyes.

There were six baggage-wagons to accompany us. They had left Salt Lake City the day before, and now rolled slowly off to precede us to Provo. Under President Young's direction, his part}' were told off to their respective vehicles, and bade farewell to the friends who had accompanied them so far. Our carriage drew up first; and I was sorry to see that it was Mr. Young's own luxurious city coach, whose springs he had devoted to be shattered over the lava blocks in my invalid husband's service. Inside, it was so piled up with cushions and fur robes, that it was almost impossible to feel a jolt. Its handsomely-varnished outside panels were protected by clean white canvas. What a red-stained, shabby covering reached the end of our seven-hundred-miles' journey!

Behind us followed a carriage containing one of Mr. Young's married daughters, a pale, bronchitic-looking young lady, traveling for her health under the care of a Mrs. Young, who was returning to her home in a southern settlement. Beside them rode Mrs. Young's fair-haired little daughter, Mabel, and many a chorus she and my boys sang from their respective perches as we toiled on our journey afterwards.

Next followed the carriage of Lorenzo Dow Young, a younger brother of the president, with his bright-eyed, sunburnt wife, alert and erect as a young woman, and a manly son of fourteen, their perfectly-reliable driver. After theirs, came various other vehicles, containing the superintendent of telegraphing in Utah, with his pretty wife; a blue-eyed, white-headed bishop from Pennsylvania — a Mormon bishop, I mean — and three or four other gentlemen in their own carriages, who were to accompany President Young for the remainder of the trip.

Not least, in his own estimation, followed a "colored gemman," an importation to Utah from Philadelphia, whose airs and ailments were henceforward to engross to distraction the time of the kind-hearted elder who withdrew him from the teamsters' company to give him a seat in his own carriage.

When the last vehicle had started. President Young stepped into his own light coupe, which carried him at a brisk trot to his place at the head of the line.

Our afternoon drive to Provo followed the margin of Utah or Timpanogos Lake, a shining sheet of fresh water, which came into view when the exigencies of the landscape demanded. Near its shore were several flourishing villages, appearing in the distance as large fruit-orchards, with detached dwellings scattered through them. Hardly any "clapboarded" houses are to be seen in Utah. The Mormons have an ugly, English-looking, burnt brick; but adobe ("dobies") or unburnt brick is most commonly used. I prefer the adobe — its general tint is of a soft dove-color, which looks well under the trees. Sometimes the Mormons coat the adobe walls with plaster of Paris, which, in their dry climate, seems to adhere permanently. Its dazzling whiteness commends it to the housekeeper's, if not to the artist's, eye. The walls of the best houses in Provo were white or light-colored, and, with their carved wooden window-dressings and piazzas and corniced roofs, looked trim as if fresh from the builder's hand.

We entered the grounds of one of the handsomest of them, a villa built in that American-Italian style which Downing characterizes as indicating "varied enjoyments, and a life of refined leisure," On its broad piazza our hostess stood ready to greet us; a buxom, black-haired, quick-eyed dame, who gave us a becoming welcome, and hailed the rest of the party with many a quip and merry jest as she led the way into her large parlor. In two minutes she had flitted up the stairway to show me my rooms; in two more she had committed my entertainment, so far as talking to me went, to another of her husband's wives, also a guest; and in about fifteen more she had all of our large party seated at a table, which was so abundantly spread that there was no more than room left for our plates. To be sure — New England fashion — we had, bier and little, glass and china, about nine apiece.

We had a brave long grace before meat. I noticed that before uttering jt President Young's eye had wandered over the table, and seen every cover lifted, even the glass top of the butter-dish. The stoppers were taken from the decanters of home-made wine. (I once saw, at a Mormon dinner-party in the city, the corks drawn from the champagne-bottles, which effervesced an accompaniment to the speaker!)

I don't know why the covers were taken off; it would have made an epicure wish the grace — a full-fledged prayer; — shorter, with such savory viands cooling.

What had we for dinner? What had we not! Turkey and beef, fresh salmon-trout from the lake, wild duck, chicken-pie, apple-fritters, wild-plum, cranberry-, and currant-jellies, a profusion of vegetables; and then mince-pies (drawn from the oven *after* the grace was said!), smoking plum-puddings for *us,* and wholesome plain ones for the children (who preferred the *un*wholesome!); pears, peaches, apples, and grapes, pitchers of cream and scarcely less creamy milk, cakes, preserves, and tarts numberless, and tea and coffee. All were served and pressed upon us by our active hostess, for whom a seat was reserved at President Young's right hand — to which she was invited about once in five minutes, replying, "Immediately, Brother Young," "Directly, Sister Lucy," as she flew off to reappear with some fresh dainty.

Such a busy woman! That she looked well to the ways of her household, no one could doubt who heard her prompt, cheery replies to the queries addressed her from time to time by President Young and her husband (he was also a guest, if a man can be a guest under his wife's roof!) respecting the welfare of the cows, and calves, and sheep, and hired boys, the winter's provision of wood and coal, and the results of the summer's husbandry.

She conducted me over her house afterward, with a justifiable pride in its exquisite neatness and the well-planned convenience of its arrangements. She showed me its porte-cochère for stormy weather, its covered ways to barn and wood-shed, and the never-failing stream of running water that was conducted through kitchen and dairy. I noticed the plump feather-beds in the sleeping-rooms, the shining blackness of the stoves (each with its tea-kettle of boiling water), that no speck dimmed her mirrors, and not a stray thread littered her carpets. It was not only here, but everywhere else in Utah, that I rejoiced in the absence of — well — spittoons, and of the necessity for them. I saw neither smoking nor chewing among the Mormons.

This Provo house was the very foppery of cleanliness. Small wonder that, with but one young girl to help her, its mistress had little leisure for reading. I had asked for books, meaning to judge of the character of the household by their aid. There was only the Bible, the Book of Mormon, a photograph album, and Worcester's Dictionary in all that big house — except in a carefully-locked closet, where were the story- and lesson-books of her one child, a son, gone now to Salt Lake City to study a profession. When she opened this door and lovingly handled the volumes, speaking of her loneliness without him, tears gathered in her eyes. I thought myself of a home that I knew of, not half so tidy it must be confessed, overflowing with books and music, playthings, and children's happy voices, where boys and girls gathered round their mother with their paintings, drawing, and sewing, while their father read aloud; and my own tears came as I thought how solitary her life must be when each day's work was done; how much more solitary it would be when the evening of her life closed in. No "John Anderson" to be her fireside companion, none of the comfort that even a lonely widow finds in the remembrance of former joys and sorrows shared with the one to whom she has been best and nearest. This woman would have only her model house, so clean and so white, so blank and vacant — even of memories!

However, my pity seemed for the present uncalled for. My hostess was soon jesting with her guests. I must admit that she appeared to be a happy and contented woman.

Our evening passed very quietly. President Young was suffering from a severe cold attended with fever, and the household retired early. While we were sitting in the long parlor he fell asleep before the fire, and the traveling party broke up into groups who chatted in low tones with the visitors who came in. When I went up-stairs after tea to put my boys safely to bed in their unfamiliar quarters, I had to draw down the window-blind to shut out the dazzling moonlight which kept them awake.

The town seemed asleep, except in the direction of the red-lit windows of a great meetinghouse whither the elders of our company had repaired, and whence I could hear distant singing. The mountains which shelter the town were distinctly visible: their snowy tops like fixed white clouds; the hill-terrace at their foot, called Provo Bench, lying black in their shadow above the town.

When I went down-stairs to take my leave for the night, I remarked to a guest, who was still lingering in the parlor, upon the extreme beauty of the scene; and she detained me until she could narrate me a "nice story" to associate with it when I returned to my moonlit rooms.

She said that in the early days of the settlement, her brother-in-law, Charles Decker, came there by appointment to "trade" with the great Ute chief Wah-ker or Wakarra. Wah-ker was the terror of the country, in his day, having undisputed range over the region: from Utah through Arizona, into California. It pleased his highness to declare that the Great Spirit had ordered him to be friends with the Mormons. To prove his friendship, he brought them property for sale, which he could not dispose of to other purchasers. His Utes would often take infant captives from the weaker Indian tribes, who were heavy stock upon their hands: and these, Wah-ker would, with a mock-sober pretence of generosity, insist upon the Mormons buying.

When Wah-ker announced that he was coming with his band to trade, the Mormons hastened to buy what they must and get rid of their dangerous friend; as in a neighborless country-house the women hasten to buy, from the boisterous drunken peddler, wares enough to relieve them of his presence.

The Mormons were not allowed to buy Indian children for *slaves*. Believing them to be Lamanites, fellow-descendants of Israel, [2] like themselves, though under a curse, they felt bound to adopt them into their families and treat them like their own children. Therefore, it was a costly purchase that Wah-ker invited them to make; and on this occasion, Decker and his comrades bought what the Indians had brought of other wares, such as dressed skins and ponies and Mexican saddles, but declined the human goods.

Wah-ker then produced a shivering little four-year-old girl, whom he insisted on their buying. He asked an extravagant price, "because he had brought her so far; away from the Santa Clara country." Her "board" could not have cost the hero much, for he used to picket his little captives "to a stake by a rope around their necks," and for days at a time they had literally nothing to eat more than was afforded them by "the run of their teeth" among the undergrowth within the length of their tether.

The Mormons were willing to pay a rifle, and even to throw in a blanket to boot, but explained that they honestly had no more goods with them than were left on the trading-ground. On this, Wah-ker became enraged, and seizing the child by her feet, whirled her in the air, dashed her down, and then, as she lay quivering out her life, he snatched his hatchet from his belt and chopped her into five pieces. "Now, you can have her at no price," he said.

The narrator considered her story ended here, but I asked, "Well, what happened then?"

"Happened?" she echoed. "Why, nothing. After Wah-ker's temper was spent, he went oft quite pleasant and dignified."

"But Decker, — your brother-in-law! Did Mr. Decker do nothing?"

"He did try to jump out of his wagon and rush on Wah-ker, but his friends held him— held his arms, till he came to himself and cooled down. What *could* four men do against two hundred and fifty?"

I did not reply. I suppose the Mormons could have achieved nothing; but I think the story of the unpunished crime affected me more than it would have done if the child's death had been avenged.

The Indian stories I have heard, when they are true, don't end prettily. No god in a machine comes down to avert the stroke of fate. The witnesses look on like the chorus in a Greek tragedy. I suppose the ancients described reality; but our modern novelists and playwrights must suit the taste of the day by bringing every story to a happy end.

Wah-ker himself died in the Pah-vant country, and the Utes made great lamentation over him. There is a narrow canon with steep rocky walls, which we saw afterwards near Kanosh's village. In one of its recesses they walled up the chief's body with loose stones, that permitted the air and some rays of light to penetrate. They killed there in his honor seven head of cattle, a Pi-ede squaw and child, captives, and then walled up with him a live Pi-ede boy. The Pah-vants, who are a race friendly to the whites, living quietly on a little reservation near, were sorry for the child. One half-breed went up at night and talked with him, but dared not be seen in daylight. After three days the little fellow could no longer restrain his cries of terror, his horror of the rotting corpse, his pangs of hunger and thirst. The fourth night there was only a moan in answer to the friendly voice; and the fifth night, silence.

[1] Yet the Mormon publications denied polygamy as late as 1852.
[2] "Those are the ten tribe's, which were carried away prisoners out of their own land in the time of Osea, the king; whom Shalmaneser, the king of Assyria, led away captive. And he carried them over the waters, and so came they into another land. They took this counsel among themselves, that they would leave the multitude of the heathen, and go forth into a further country, where never mankind dwelt. That they might there keep their statutes, which they never kept in their own land. Then dwelt they there until the latter time." — II. Esdras, xiii. 40-46.

Payson

Looking from my window at Provo, that night, I had remarked a great building that looked in the distance like a fortress. We visited it next morning and found it'-nothing more formidable than a large woolen factory, not yet in operation. It is to run 270 spindles, and make a variety of cloths. The superintendent proved to be a nephew of the Brothers Kelly, of Kellyville, in Pennsylvania, and I felt as if he were quite an old acquaintance in this outlandish corner of the world, though I only know his relatives' Mills by sight when I am at home.

We left Provo that afternoon, in spite of President Young's evident indisposition. I asked a lady of the party whether some one would not urge his staying a day longer to recruit his strength.

"No," she replied, stiffly; "he will be inspired to do right. If he *ought* to go, we will know it by his going; if not, he will be inspired to stay. He is guided by the spirit in every action of his life."

Payson was our next stage from Provo. The very pretty daughter of our host here was the child of an only wife. He admitted his single-blessedness with the half-shamefaced laugh that in our country might have followed the announcement that a lady was his third spouse. Third, vertically, I mean, as L. M. used to say of Bishop H.'s matrimonial series. I did not think that Mrs. Angus seemed likely to urge a second wife upon her lord; since, for anything that I could see, he throve financially as well as if he had fulfilled all the conditions of saintship. He was one of the few Irish Mormons whom I met (indeed, *Scotch*-Irish at that). His house was a large adobe which had grown with his prosperity, for it had been added to three times, and included a flourishing millinery establishment conducted by Mrs. Angus. It had two well-furnished parlors; one in particular with a conspicuously costly carpet. Fires were blazing in both; but I think quite as comfortable a room was a long kitchen where we ate our meals. Like all Mormon living-rooms, it was virtuously clean and well-aired. Trailing plants climbed round the windows, and as the sunshine poured in, a canary tried to outsing the tones of Brigham Young's grace. He held his own, however; and would not have its cage covered, maintaining that the bird's effusion of thankfulness might be as acceptable to the Creator as his own.

At every one of the places we stayed on this journey, we had prayers immediately after the dinner-supper, and prayers again before breakfast. No one was excused; wives, daughters, hired men and women, all shuffled in. The Mormons do not read from the Bible, but kneel at once, while the head of the household or an honored guest prays aloud, beginning, as I noticed on this occasion, instead of ending, "In the name of Thy Son, our Saviour Jesus Christ, Father, we ask," etc. I do not think they as often say, "If it be Thy Will," as we do, but simply pray for the blessings they want, expecting they will be given or withheld, as God knows best. Though I do remember Brigham Young's once praying for the restoration and healing of the sick "if not appointed unto death." They spend very little time in ascriptions, but ask for what they need and thank Him for what He has given — with surprising fluency and detail.

It interested me and my children, too, though they could scarcely repress a start and titter, when they and their absent brother and sister were alluded to by name. At home, when, for no greater audience than my children, I venture to extemporize the prayer at family worship. I am sometimes puzzled whether to introduce the names of individuals, or to adhere prudently to generalities. But the Mormons take it for granted that God knows our familiar names and tides, and will ask a blessing on

"Thy servant, Colonel Jonathan P. Hitchcock, Jr.," where I would spend a minute or two in devising a periphrasis. I liked this when I became used to it, and could join in with some knowledge of the circumstances of those we prayed for; particularly as the year drew on, and the whole people were in suspense awaiting the action of Congress affecting them.

After leaving Payson we rounded the head of Utah Lake, and climbed slowly up the gentle ascent between its basin and Juab Valley. The ground over which we traveled was strewn with cobble-stones, with here and there a deep pool of clear water. Such pools abound in this part of Utah, and many of them are considerably larger than they appear to the passer-by. The margin is overgrown by a coarse, strong grass, whose roots mat together and gradually encroach upon the surface, forming, in time, a floating edge, strong enough to bear a man. Cattle, however, coming down to drink, overweight it, and falling in, are frequently drowned. My attention was called to three particularly, stated by a sworn accuser of the Mormons to have been selected by him for conducting certain choice *noyades* ordered by Brigham Young. To believe the story, the dead thrown into these pools rose to the surface of the water, and rolled round -and round for weeks!

My husband assured me that the Juab Valley was a charming green plain in summer, and pointed out that even now in December it was dotted with herds of cattle among the sage-brush. But I could not imagine its possible loveliness at any season.

At a doleful-looking ranch, Panyan Springs, where we paused to let. our horses drink, a group of teamsters had kindled a fire, and stood warming themselves over it. Among them was our servant, his natural ebony turned clay-color by the icy wind that came rushing down from Mount Nebo's 12,000 feet of altitude. One of my boys who is of a poetic turn, pointed it out to John, meaning to say, "Grand!" "Yes, indeed," shivered John, "Dreadful!" The snowy peaks of this glorious mountain glistened on our horizon day after day, until we crossed the Rim of the Basin.

At another watering-place, Santaquin, I think, somewhat above the general level of the plain, we saw quite a number of white-topped wagons slowly toiling along the dusty track below us. Some lighter ones turned aside, as we ourselves frequently did, to drive through the aromatic sage-brush. It scarcely afforded more obstruction to the wheels than grass would have done. But while we were standing at a watering-trough, up rolled one of the coaches of the Gilmore Stage line. I noticed the half-tipsy mirth on the countenances of the driver and of the two red-faced passengers, who were leaning out of the window watching his movements. By a skilfully-given pull of the reins, he steered his heavy wagon right against the hub of our front wheel, and then drove off laughing. Unfortunately for the joke, however, the villagers beyond stopped his team, and he came back, crestfallen, to apologize. It was undoubtedly meant as an insult to the Mormon leader, in whose well-known carriage, however, the only Gentiles of the party happened to be seated. President Young received his excuses with dignity, instead of "blowing him up," as a more impetuous friend of mine was ready to do. Our carriage was examined, and pronounced still fit for work; but it took some hours at our next stopping - place to repair the damage. The people of the village complained that this was a favorite amusement of the coaches near this point, where the Mormon travel coincides with that of the Nevada mining regions.

Among the groups gathered around the carriages, many eagerly claimed T.'s recognition. A sturdy yellow-haired man, thrusting both his sinewy brown hands through the carriage window, shook T.'s hand and mine and the children's, all at once, it seemed.

"My dear," says T. to me, "this is my old friend, Lot Smith. You know *him* well by name!"

I tried very hard to look as if I did; but T., with all his virtues, sometimes puts me in an embarrassing position by introducing me with the same form of words to some "old friend," whose name he has clean forgotten, and trusts I shall find out Incidentally for him. *Now,* he had the name; but whether he remembered anything more, I doubted. "Lot Smith, Lot Smith?" Naturally, being in Utah, my thoughts flew to the late Joseph, and I mentally enumerated the scions of that house, whose photographs had been brought us by his gigantic young kinsman, Samuel. No; there was no *Lot* among them.

"And so you are content to be a quiet farmer at 'Bountiful'?" T. was saying, as I gave up my researches among the Smiths.

"And so *you* are contented to be a quiet citizen since you came back from the wars?" retorted the other. "No, indeed. Colonel. I'm just waitin' the word. I'm expectin' to hear of that there expedition to the Arctics, and when you're ready *I* am. We'll have real times like you had in the snows out by Bridger in '58."

Oh, to be sure! Now I had him! In '57, when the government army trains were stampeded and wagons burnt, it was Lot Smith who was accused of being the hero of the attack. And this thick-set, steady-looking farmer was the same man of whom I had heard a story that I could applaud more.

When he was a member of the Mormon battalion in Mexico or Lower California, he put down a bull-fight.

He told the Spaniards that it was an exhibition as cowardly as it was cruel, and that if they wanted to show their pluck, they shouldn't kill the bull, but ride it.

"No man may ride a maddened bull!" said the Dons.

"One man will!" he retorted. And leaping on the neck of a bellowing quadruped they had just brought in, he rode it round the ring, holding on by its horns, until a favoring toss landed him in the canopied box of the alcalde's family.

As we drove on, T. told me of other adventures of Lot's; but I was weary and depressed, and they made little impression on my mind.

The scattered settlements hereabout looked poor, and more in the Irish mud-cabin style than those we had passed before; yet the wide, unpaved streets were bordered with cottonwoods, and each house was set in its ample orchard of young fruit-trees, while water flowed through irrigating channels, suggesting the expenditure of much patient toil before the plantations had been successful.

Each Mormon settlement has its open central square; in the later ones unfenced, but in the earlier surrounded by a crumbling wall of adobe and cobble-stone, the quondam "fort," or "corral," for protection against Indians. In the poorer settlements their assemblages for religious or patriotic purposes (with the Mormons convertible terms) are still held in great open sheds, roofed only with woven boughs, called "boweries," which stand in the midst of these central squares. Even now, though the people say they are safe from Indians, I noticed that the tithing and farm-yards were enclosed by walls or strong wattled fences or stockades.

The hay-stacks in the dry, pure air had taken a bright straw-color outside, but where they were cut down into for the cattle, were of a green almost as fresh as that of new-mown grass. Sometimes the hay was not piled in stacks, but laid upon a stout pole framework, so as to form the roof and sides of a shelter for the cattle against the wind,

I know — that is I have been told — that the scenery between Payson and Nephi is tine, — that mountains near and distant were keeping up with us all the way. But I can't say that I appreciated it. The behavior of the rude men at Santaquin had put me out of temper; my lot in life having previously been cast where such insolence in a lady's presence would not have escaped chastisement. And, as generally happens in such moods, I gave most attention to the sights most immediately under our carriage windows. Now the wheels ran noiselessly; and now they jolted roughly over coarse pebbles and gravel. The sky clouded over, too; and its dull gray met the gray of the uninteresting plain, with its unvarying shabby growth of wormwood, no twig of which seems to have a natural termination, but to have been bent round and twisted or bitten off.

Towards nightfall, as our weary horses dragged us on to the close of the long day's journey, hills we had seen in the distance ahead began to tower up tall mountains; hiding still higher snowy peaks beyond. A cluster of houses and fenced gardens lying in their shelter was pointed out as Nephi. We saw smokes away up on one of the heights above the town, which T. said were probably Indian fires; and the children and I felt, with quickened pulse, that we were nearing the pass into treacherous "Tab-i-yuna's" country.

Nephi

I could see little of Nephi in the gathering darkness: it was evidently smaller than Provo. The carriages halted on entering the town, and separated company. Ours was driven rapidly up a cross-street to a plain adobe house, standing by itself. Lights shone from every door and window; the father of the family stood waiting to help us out of the carriage, and the wives and children greeted us warmly as we crossed the threshold.

We were first ushered into a large bedroom on the ground floor, where a superb pitch-pine fire was blazing; and two well-cushioned rocking-chairs were drawn forward for us, while half a dozen hospitable children took off my boys' wrappings, as the mother disembarrassed me of mine.

Then we were left to rest, and begged to feel ourselves at home.

Our present entertainers, the Steerforths, were English people. There were *two* wives, and a number of children, girls of all sizes down to the smallest elf that ever walked, and one sturdy open-faced boy, who speedily "fellow-shipped" with my little lads, and carried them off, after supper, to the great kitchen to see their playmate, Lehi, the Indian boy.

After supper! — To this day, when we have any special dainty at home, Evan and Will exclaim that it reminds them of the Steerforths', and describe the cozy dining-room, with the warm fire-light playing on the table-equipage, and the various good things' that composed, in Yorkshire style, the hungry little travelers' "tea-dinner."

One of the wives sat down to table, and one waited upon us, with the aid of the two elder girls. There was a young schoolmaster there, too, who had made his home with the Steerforths since his parents died, and whose love of their quiet domestic life was duly praised by the Mistresses S. when he left the room. But I thought that the sweet face of "our eldest" — "Noe," I think they call her — might perhaps share the credit of the long ten-mile ride on Friday evening from his school to Nephi, and the starlight journey back which it cost the youthful pedagogue on Monday morning.

My intercourse with the Steerforths made a strong impression on me. We stayed longer at their house than at any other on this tour, and it was difficult not to be influenced by their simple kindliness of heart and unaffected enthusiasm.

Our conversation the evening of our arrival turned chiefly on our hostesses' experience of pioneer life. Mrs. Mary was the chief speaker, but Mrs. Sarah, a pale little lady, dark-haired and black-eyed, put in a quiet word of acquiescence, or suggested an anecdote now and then. She was from Yorkshire. Mrs. Mary was a Herefordshire woman, tall, rosy, brown-haired, and blue-eyed.

I wonder whether the Mormon men evince any marked peculiarity of taste in the selection of wives. Widowers with us are wont to profess that they discern a resemblance in the lady upon whom a second choice falls, to the dear departed. I asked a Mormon woman at Salt Lake how it was, and she answered that, in her opinion, men had no taste. "In our case," she said, "there are *five* of us unusually tall, and *two* very short; but the rest (she did not say how many there were) are of an ordinary height, and we are all different in looks, disposition, and age."

In the Steerforth ménage, the wives were exceedingly unlike each other. The husband was of a Manx family, long resident in Yorkshire. He had joined the Mormons in early youth with his mother, and they had been disowned by his family, well-to-do English people. He had prospered so well in Utah, however, that the family had now made overtures of reconciliation, and a bachelor "Uncle Lillivick" was coming to make Nephi a visit.

The Steerforths were among the first Mormons who came out to Utah. Only a select band of one hundred and forty-three men, headed by Brigham Young in person, had preceded them. These pioneers had planted posts along their route with rough boxes nailed to them, containing information regarding the distances to wood, water, and grass; and these guide-posts were slowly tracked out and followed by the long train of ox-wagons, freighted with the exiles from Nauvoo, women, children, and invalids. There were a few men who drove and acted as guards, but the teamsters were principally women and young boys.

Our government had invited the Mormons, as a test of their loyalty, Mrs. Mary said, to furnish volunteers for the war then going on with Mexico. The Mormons raised a battalion, five hundred strong containing most of the young men who should have escorted the helpless ones; and they were gone twenty months, reaching Salt Lake Valley, she told me, from the then almost unknown California. Some found that their wives and infants had perished from the sufferings they had undergone; others found them established in tiny homes, longingly awaiting him.

I asked Mrs. Mary whether the band of exiles knew where they were to go. Had the pioneers returned?

"No," she said; "we heard from time to time how they were faring, from the post-office boxes, but that was all we knew."

"Were you long on the journey?"

"Very long," she said; "but we kept cheerful, knowing the Lord was our guide. But you can think what we felt when we came into the mountains, and word was passed one day from wagon to wagon, that Brother Young and the other pioneers were in sight, coming back to meet us! They brought news that they had chosen the spot for us to settle, and planted seed-corn there. It was beautiful weather, and we had a dance, and prayers, and songs of thankfulness that night, by the light of the moon."

"Were you able to use the corn they had planted?" I asked.

"No; we saved it for next year, as far as we could. We brought some with us, and ground it up at a rough little mill we had on City Creek. I wore out five veils sifting flour. At first we set aside what would not pass through; but we were glad to use it all, with the bran, long before the new harvest was gathered."

"Did you suffer from famine when you first entered the Valley?" I inquired.

"No," she answered, "not exactly. We always had something to eat, though the poor children used" to long for the time when they might eat as hearty a meal as they wanted. We had to reckon so closely how much we could allow for each meal, that we never rose up from one with our hunger satisfied. But as there was no variety of food, our appetites were less tempted. Where the water was good, we drank a good deal of it; where it was not, we boiled it. With a little milk we could make cambric tea, which was found to be one of the best of remedies for hunger — taken hot, and with a little spice or aromatic herbs to flavor it."

"I call *that* suffering."

"Not what a Mormon would call by the name," answered little Mrs. Sarah's quiet voice. "Mary," she added, "tell Mrs. T. about the dark days; tell her of the winter before."

"I can never call them our dark days, sister," she rejoined. "We were starving, we were dying, suffering was then consuming life itself; but it was that which gave its brightness to the flame. The flame of true religion was burning then. God was with this People. I would give a thousand days of the present luxury and folly, for one hour of that exalted life."

She said this and more, with a voice expressive of deep emotion. I did not understand what wrong key I had struck; but I turned back the dialogue.

"When was it that you got enough at last?" I asked.

"Well," she said, "in August, 1848, a year after the pioneers came out, when the first harvest of the Salt Lake farms was gathered in, we made a great day of rejoicing before the Lord. We had long tables set out in the open air, under 'boweries;' and all the women and girls were busy baking, broiling, stewing, and roasting. Every stranger in the settlement (and there were a good many on their way to California) was made welcome to as much as he could eat; and then in the evening we had dancing and singing that lasted all night. We dismissed all care for the time, and made it a day of pure thanksgiving. We had to pinch somewhat after that, but the worst was over. Our family did not stay very long in the valley, for Mr.

Steerforth was one of the first appointed to come down here to Salt Creek."

"Why do you call this place Salt Creek?" I asked.

"Our creek water *is* salt. There is a salt mountain up the cañon, and there is a good deal sold from here; and, of course, the Gentiles don't like to use our names for places, when they can use others and be understood."

I inquired about the smokes that we had seen above Nephi as we approached, and Mrs. Mary said that they *were* kindled by Indians. They had been there two days.

"Are you not afraid?"

"Oh, no; the Indians are perfectly friendly now."

"How long is it since they harmed any one belonging to your settlement?"

"Well," she answered, tranquilly, "no one to speak of, these three months, and then it was only one man — Brother Hart — who was out alone, against counsel. It was last October. He went up the canon to haul down some firewood, taking his little boy along. The valley is very narrow, and in some places rocks overhang the road. The Indians fired right down upon him. They wounded the boy, too, but he escaped. Probably they wanted the horses only, for they could have caught Phineas if they had tried."

"Do you suppose they had any special motive," I inquired, "beyond coveting the horses?"

"Brother Hart had had stock stolen, and was known by the Indians to be vexed about it. He has left a widow, poor fellow, and young children."

A visitor remarked that it was Tab-i-yuna who was supposed to have killed Brother Hart, and that Kanosh, the friendly Pah-vant chief, accused Tab-i-yuna of it.

Mrs. Sarah said that their family had twice been compelled to move off in former times by the Indians, and often to "go into the Fort," but they felt perfectly safe, since the new San Pete settlements intervened between them and Tab-i-yuna. Now I had heard before leaving Salt Lake, that Tab-i-yuna had threatened war unless black-mail was paid; and from better authority than Mrs. Steerforth had access to, that this had been refused. I had learned, too, that there was an entirely undefended pass between his country and Nephi, but I thought it kindest not to alarm my hostesses with my fears.

Both women then went on to tell me of a visit Tab-i-yuna had made Nephi in the summer with his band.

We have heard our English friends with country-places, complain of the gypsies strolling through the country, camping here and there, and pilfering from friend or foe. But their grievance is a bagatelle compared to that the Mormons endure, under the infliction of a visit from a party of Indians. They have the appetites of poor relations, and the touchiness of rich ones with money to leave. They come in a swarm; their ponies eat down the golden grain-stacks to their very centres; the Mormon women are tired out baking for the masters, while the squaws hang about the kitchens watching for scraps like unpenned chickens.

"The women are glad enough, poor creatures," cried pretty Noe, "of a chance to carry water or do any drudge work to repay us for gentle treatment; but the men — the insolent young braves and warriors, who expect the sisters to wait on them, and never thank us by a look — I wonder how mother and the rest Can stand it."

"They often mean better than they are able to show," pleaded Mrs. Mary. "I had an old Shoshoné squaw, the wife of Baptiste, the Ute medicine-man," she continued, turning to me, "who washed for us for several years, and was as honest as the day. One morning she came in from the mountains, kissed the children and cried over them, and made signs that we must all *go*, and seemed as if she was in terror of being seen or overheard, yet anxious to make us promise to leave. We did not understand why she was so earnest, for the report was that the Indians were quiet.

"We 'had had a regular guard out for some time then, for there had been Indian alarms in the summer; but as we understood that no hostile Indians were near, their vigilance had relaxed. Still, the men never went afield without carrying their guns. The day before old Peggy called, one had left his gun while he went to drink at a brook. He had seen nobody either going or coming back, but he found two arrows had been fixed crosswise between the ramrod and the barrel of his gun, to show how near some one had crept to him. Such warnings were often given by friendly Indians, to show us how little we guessed their nearness; but half the time our people did not understand their meaning, and they dared not impart it to us more plainly.

"It happened," she went on, "that the next day was Sunday. I could not go to meeting, having a bad headache. As I sat by the window reading my Bible, I saw Indians come stealing by until they completely surrounded the church. They were all armed, and I was too much terrified to leave my seat, either to hide myself or to make an effort to warn the congregation. Baptiste was leader of the band; and after a few minutes he stripped and danced into the church naked."

"Oh!" I exclaimed, involuntarily, "what did he do that for?"

"I wondered, too," she answered; "but I learned that it was done to banter them — that is," she explained, replying to my look of interrogation — "to insult them by indecent behavior, and make them turn him out. That would have given him an excuse to work himself and his band into a fighting rage. That's the way with the poor creatures, you know. Some of their grandest warriors seem to need to work themselves up into a kind of hysterical passion, before they are brave enough to attack our people when they affect not to mind them.

"Baptiste was disappointed. One of the brethren sitting near a window bethought himself to look out, and seeing the Indians, warned the rest. So they took no notice of Baptiste; but continued the services, only singing a little louder in the hymn parts, perhaps; and. Baptiste stood awhile, then sat down, and then stole out, and took his band away.

"Some say," she interrupted herself with a smile, "that he thought that a great 'medicine' was going on, and considering himself a brother of the craft, withdrew from courtesy.

"Whatever his motive was, we took it as a warning; the settlers were all moved into the Fort; and three days after, the biggest Indian war we ever had in the territory, broke out. Some of our dearest friends were its earliest victims."

I had heard in Salt Lake City of the power of Baptiste's "medicine," and observing the interest my questions evinced in the subject, the Steerforths brought round to me a neighbor, who had been an eye-witness of one of his performances. I think I have from him a reliable circumstantial account of the transaction of a Ute pow-wow cure.'

According to this citizen's relation, he chanced to be in Wah-ker's camp when a noted Indian — I think he said Arrahpene — was taken alarmingly ill. Wah-ker despatched a man and boy to bring Baptiste. They took two ponies with them, and left the camp at three in the morning for Baptiste's lodge, fifty miles off. Half way there the man halted with one of the ponies, sending the boy on with the other. Baptiste and his squaw, carrying a "bag of needments," made such good speed with the aid of the pony relays that they reached Wah-ker's camp before sunset.

Baptiste entered the sick man's lodge alone; but several persons, and among them my informant, peeped in through the opening between the skins; and, after Baptiste's attention was absorbed in his patient, they stole inside the lodge. Arrahpene lay on the ground in a stupor, seeming to take no notice of the conjuror.

Baptiste now took from his bag sundry nondescript articles, which he hung solemnly upon a pole, and kindled a fire of sticks in the centre of the lodge, on which, from time to time, he threw a powder from his pouch, which made a noisome smell. He then began walking round and round his patient, as the mesmerists are said to do, always keeping his old witch's face toward him. But, as if finding them of no avail, he threw himself suddenly upon Arrahpene, clasped him round the body, and rolled him from side to side. At this exercise he persevered until the spectators grew tired of watching him.

At intervals he would jump up, chanting a tuneless, windy song, and snatch at one of the magic rags he had hung to the lodge-pole, appearing not to notice that he stepped through the burning fire to reach it. After this he stroked his hands now down his own sides, and now down Arrahpene's. Once more he threw himself on the body, — this time as if he wanted to squeeze the life out. Then he swallowed a bit of thick, red flannel, and after each few minutes spat it up, examined it as it lay in his palm, swallowed it again, after shaking his head, and resumed the rolling. Presently he divested himself of all his clothing, both the sick man and himself being bathed in perspiration, and the invalid showing other signs that life was coming back to him in force. Again and again he swallowed and threw up the bit of red flannel, and muttered over it, and again and again rolled on the sick man, still singing his queer song, and jumping up at intervals to fumble with the "medicine" rags.

At last it was over; a final diagnosis of the red flannel, changed to a repulsive, slimy mass, satisfied him. He 'turned, angrily kicked aside the ashes of the fire, scraped a hole in the ground underneath, and there buried the flannel, into which the evil spirit of the disease had passed. All that remained was for him to rake the ashes over the spot again, shake himself, and resume his clothing. The tent-flap was thrown open, the fresh air let in. The sick man thereupon rose, and left the lodge with Baptiste, perfectly restored to health.

I asked my informant if he was satisfied of the genuineness of the cure. He insisted that there could be no doubt of it. "The Indians," he said, "are very superstitious, and help the efforts of their medicine-man by implicit faith in his power. But they have still more faith for our *real* miracles. Even those who have not embraced the faith, think that *our* 'medicine,' as they call 'the gifts,' is more powerful than theirs."

While I was at Nephi, I saw a Mormon "sister" who had just returned from Tab-i-yuna's camp, where she had spent several days and nights, nursing a sick squaw of his band. She was quite ill herself, from having been so long in the close air and dirt of a little skin-lodge; but her countenance lit up, and she raised her voice loud and high in announcing the creature's perfect cure to the members of the Female Relief Society. She seemed to me unreasonably elated over it. I found that it was on account of the moral effect her recovery was expected to produce on the "Lamanites."

Hitherto, Tab-i-yuna had been a most "stubborn Jew," and now, for the first time, and when they were in dread of him, he had sent, of his own accord, for the brethren, desiring them to "lay hands upon" the squaw and "minister to her." They had gladly complied, carrying the good sister with them, and leaving her with the squaw, who took a turn for the better, they said, from the time the brethren laid hands upon her.

The effect of superstitious credulity upon her mind did something, I suppose, and kind nursing did something; and I presume the Mormons were not altogether wrong in thinking that God's blessing did most of all.

Even I felt free to admit that Mormon Christianity would be a better belief than Tab i yuna's heathen superstition, or the moral law our soldiers teach in their intercourse with the Indians. Ugh! If I were a man how I would speak out against the beasts!

The Steerforths had often seen both Wah-ker and Arrahpene, his brother-in-law and successor. Old Baptiste was a relative of Wah-ker's, too, Mrs. Mary said; and then she took me into the kitchen, to see the adopted son of the family, "Lehi," one of the Pi-ede children whom Wah-ker had captured in his infancy.

Lehi sat in the warmest corner of the ruddy hearth, and the little Steerforths were coaxing him to tell my boys about his days of slavery. Like most of the Indians who have grown up in the Mormon families, he was sickly. Rheumatism, dyspepsia, and consumption seem to follow the change of diet and more sedentary life. He would not talk while I stayed there, although he looked pleased when Mrs. Steerforth promised him that T. would play for him on the violin he had bought, but had not yet learned to use. After I was gone he described to my boys how Wah-ker's band used to amuse themselves in terrifying him. Sometimes they buried the poor child up to the chin in earth, and leaving food and water just outside his reach, informed him that the band were going to move away. On other occasions, the young braves would send for him, and, telling him that the time had come to kill him, would take aim. When they found that he did not flinch, they would say he might go this time. The sweet little boys of the band, too, were allowed to exercise their infant skill in archery upon him, the game being to see how near they could come to hitting, without actually piercing, him. He showed the children the scars on his back and legs and feet, where they used to try his powers of endurance by playfully branding him with a burning stick.

No wonder that Lehi used to hide under the bed at Mrs. Steerforth's whenever an Indian came near, as the dog who has once been shot at hides from a man approaching with a gun.

Another of Wah-ker's infant captives was adopted into President Young's family. She seemed to me a very respectable and sedate, good woman, but was said to entertain a "morbid" horror of Indians. I was told that when she was sold, a young brother of hers, remaining on hand after the rest of the captives were disposed of, was thrown alive into the Boiling Spring, a mile north of Salt Lake City. President Young himself, who ought to know, I suppose, contradicts this story. He does not think it was her brother, in the first place, and, in the second, the lad was killed before he was thrown in!

I found the Mormons disposed to justify and excuse the Indians more than I thought the hideous creatures deserved; and, if Wah-ker didn't boil *that* boy alive, he committed enough atrocities to justify the terror in which his name was held among the subordinate Utes.

Mrs. Mary's Indian stories made me nervous; and on retiring to rest, after extinguishing my candle, I observed, with small satisfaction, that I was to see the Pi-ute fires distinctly through the window at the foot of my bed if I should wake at night. The thought itself kept me watching them. I fancied I could see them brighten from time to time, and felt sure that if I fell asleep I would dream of Robinson Crusoe's cannibals dancing round their flaming fagots.

Instead, I figured at two home-funerals as chief mourner! It was a relief to wake to the peacefulness of a Sunday morning, with bright sunshine streaming through the window.

After breakfast I attended a Mormon meeting for the first time. I wondered whether Mr. Steerforth would walk to church alone, or between his wives. But they both accompanied me, while their joint husband (!) formed one of a group who escorted T. So there was no test of preference like that which mocks the tomb of Lord Burleigh. We soon mingled with a stream of neatly-dressed people all going the same way; my children undevoutly rambling from one side of the road to the other. They called my attention to a tamed magpie, whose remarks the little Steerforths declared to be worth hearing. But we paused in vain; he would not show off I had not known that the magpie was a native of Utah; I had supposed him a peculiarly English bird.

We passed a heap of smouldering brands — sticks and ragged strips of cedar-bark. I had fancied that a fire of "cedarn-wood" would give out a scent like sandal-wood. The perfume resembled that of the fustiest of greasy woolen clothes, and was strong enough to poison the sweet air for quite a distance.

I got rid of more than one preconceived idea that morning; of none more completely than the prevailing error respecting the looks of a congregation of Mormon women. I was so placed that I had a good opportunity to look around, and began at once to seek for the "hopeless, dissatisfied, worn" expression travelers' books had bidden me read on their faces.

But I found that they wore very much the same countenances as the American women of any large rustic and village congregation.

As we grow older, most of us pass through trials enough to score their marks upon cheek and brow; but ill-health and ill-temper plough furrows quite as deep as guilt or misfortune. Take your own congregation, the sad histories of so many of whose members you know, and see whether you can read the tragedies of their lives beneath the composed Sunday expression their faces wear. Happy or unhappy, *I* could not read histories on the upturned faces at Nephi. I looked on old women's sunburned and wrinkled visages, half-hidden in their clean sunbonnets; decent, matronly countenances framed in big old-fashioned bonnets; bright, young eyes and rosy cheeks under coquettish round hats — you might see thousands of women resembling them in our country churches.

The irrepressible baby was present in greater force than with us, and the element young man wonderfully largely represented. This is always observable in Utah meetings.

The services differed from our own. They followed a prescribed order — I judged from the readiness with which the congregation adapted itself to them; but in a certain unceremonious manner, not irreverent, but which somehow seemed to be protesting against formalism. A number of men, bishops and elders, I suppose, sat on a large platform. On a table, covered with a white cloth, were a couple of jugs of water, two plates of bread, and a common case-knife. A small reading-desk held a plainly-bound Bible, a hymn book, and a Book of Mormon.

There was a low buzz of conversation among the crowded audience for some minutes after we took our seats. The outer door being closed, one of the bishops said, "Brethren and sisters will please come to order." Then came a prayer, then a very well-sung hymn, in which the congregation was led by a choir of fourteen; and then three or four addresses, all of a moral and practical character. There was no text given out, but occasional allusions were made to passages in either the Bible or the Book of Mormon; as, "If my memory serves me, the Bible says: I guess it is somewhere in Isaiah," so and so. They gave the sense, but not the literal rendering of the words of Scripture, as far as my memory served me.

Different speakers, all men, shared the services among them; but I could not see whether President Young arranged who should speak, or whether one of the bishops, who seemed to invite each orator to address the meeting, did so of his own accord. There were no robes, gowns, altars, flowers, or other devices to attract attention to the performances, but it seemed unnecessary. The audience seemed gravely intent upon what was said, although I noticed a distinct change of expression pass over the assembly, as a man of winning and beautiful countenance rose to speak. When he turned, he was seen to be hump-backed. We often heard him preach afterwards; and my children grew so fond of his quaint picturesque eloquence, that they were eager to go even to "week-day meeting," on the chance of hearing Elder Potto.

He began by an allusion to his deformity as a cross which he found hardest to bear when he had to face an audience. But, he said, he knew that he could not profit them if he spoke in the spirit and person of William C. Potto, and he hoped that the brethren and sisters would pray for him, that the Spirit of God might descend upon him, and speak through his feeble voice. He paused some moments: the people prayed in silence — or seemed to do so — before he went on with his address.

I wish that I had taken notes of his sermon. It turned chiefly upon the duties of children to parents. It was replete with familiar illustration, — often colloquial, and never wandering from the precepts he designed to teach, — but belonged to the class of discourses it is hard to report. He closed by a curious account of his own spiritual conversion. It began like a Methodist "experience" — became psychological: afterwards touched on the miraculous. A Mormon is never inconvenienced by his story turning on a miracle. Other speakers followed more briefly. When one of them was under full headway, he paused abruptly — as if he had been ordered to do so — and the bread was blessed in the following words, which I found afterwards were taken from the "Book of Mormon, fourth chapter of Moroni:"

"Oh God, the Eternal Father, we ask Thee, in the name of Thy Son Jesus Christ, to bless and sanctify this bread to the souls of all who may partake of it, that they may eat it in remembrance of the body of Thy Son, and witness unto Thee, Oh God the Eternal Father, that they are willing to take upon them the name of Thy Son, and always remember Him, and keep His commandments which He hath given them, that they may always have His Spirit to be with them. Amen."

The bread, already in slices, was then broken and handed to every one, children included. This occupied a long time, but the speaker had resumed his address. Then the water was blessed, thus:

"Oh God, the Eternal Father, we ask Thee, in the name of Thy Son Jesus Christ, to bless and sanctify this water to the souls of all who drink of it, that may do it in remembrance of the blood of Thy Son, which was shed for them, that they may witness unto Thee, Oh God the Eternal Father, that they do always remember Him, that they may have His Spirit to be with them. Amen!"

While the water was being handed round, another hymn was sung; one of a set of beautiful fugues of which the Mormons are particularly fond. Then the services were concluded with a blessing, and the congregation dispersed, interchanging greetings at the door.

I spent the afternoon with my two hostesses; but T. was taken to inspect a monster Sunday-school, where he found the pupils well drilled in the Bible and the Book of Mormon. The latter is a production which sounds not unlike the historical books of the Old Testament in the ears of those who "read their chapters" in the mechanical way in which an ignorant Catholic tells his beads.

While I talked with the Steerforth women over the glowing fire, I was idly wondering to which of the wives the different children belonged. The wee nursling and Noe were easily assigned to the little mother, but I puzzled myself vainly over the others who gathered about the pair with precisely the same caressing -familiarity that we are accustomed to associate with the true filial instinct one and undivided. When I mentioned, my difficulty they smiled, and asked me to point out those whom I thought belonged to each. I did so; and they laughed outright, telling me that the seven children belonged to the little mother. She had also lost five. "Aunt Mary" was childless in name, but I never saw a mother of whom children seemed to be fonder, or who took more pride in the promising future of her natural offspring.

It was she who followed me to my room the first night, and, while she saw to my comfort, gave me incidental anecdotes in praise of "our girls." The bed-hangings were trimmed with finely-knitted lace, and, assuming it to be her own work, I had complimented her upon it in the morning.

She disclaimed it: "Sister Sarah really is wonderful handy, but I have no turn that way." Next morning she apologized for her sister-wife's absence from the breakfast-room: "The baby breaks her rest so much at night, that the only thing to preserve her health is to let her lie late in the morning. The girls, particularly Mary, are so useful; they can prepare the meal with very little assistance from, me."

Sunday afternoon, when the little mother happened to be talking with unusual energy, she brought little Mercy's head into violent contact with the stove-pipe. She looked distressed, and tried vainly to soothe it for a few minutes, but then laid the infant, without a word, in Aunt Mary's offered arms, where it nestled down in a way that showed it was used to being cosseted there.

The pair then pointed out to me the comfort, to a simple family, that there was in having two wives to lighten the labors and duties of the household, giving me a number of instances in proof.

Mrs. Mary further spoke of the friendship that existed between such sister-wives, as a closer tie than could be maintained between the most intimate friends living in different circumstances. "Even sisters by blood," she said, "are parted, when they marry, by new interests independent of each other; and, fond as may be the affection that remains, the bond of daily habit and propinquity is broken. But, in our home, each of us has a friend whose interests are identical with her own, who can share all the joys and troubles of the family, and to whom she can impart her feelings regarding its head without fear of violating that sacred confidence which may not be shared with any outside friend."

Can you imagine anything sober — more insane? I listened with perfect composure. I was under no temptation to laugh, with those two poor ladies looking into my face inquiringly, even when they spoke most confidently of their solution of life's problems. — "The pity of it, Iag-o!"

The Steerforths were the first Mormon women who awakened sympathy in my breast, dissociated from an equally strong feeling of repulsion; but afterwards, even when I was thrown among the Mormon Doras and Mrs. Nicklebys, in their absurd prattle about their family relations some chord of nature would be struck which moved anything but a smile.

One day, in Salt Lake City, I chanced to remark to a visitor that I had just seen a funeral pass my window.

"Yes," she answered, "it was young Mrs. R.'s. She was a sweet little creature. Did you know her?"

"No," I said; "whose daughter was she?"

Mrs. D, mentioned the name, — one well known to me, — and continued: "She and her husband grew up little boy- and girl-lovers; were engaged when she was thirteen, and married when she was sixteen, and now she is dead at seventeen, leaving a baby a few days old."

"Poor little baby!" said I. "Who is there to take care of it?"

"Oh, the baby will do very well," Mrs. D. replied; "her mother will clothe and tend it; and, fortunately, her father's second wife had a baby the very day Mrs. R. died, and she has undertaken to suckle both children. Yes, the baby will do very well, — it's the husband I pity."

My heart not being very soft towards the woes of Mormon widowers, I hinted that perhaps the man would soon find consolation in another marriage.

"Of course he will marry," she replied, gravely; "but that's not it. I think a man who loses his partner is so much more helpless than a woman. Of all the forlorn creatures, I think a man that has lost a wife is the forlornest. Like a hen with its head off, you know, Mrs. T. He don't know what to do for himself, nor for the children. There's my husband, now (a man twenty-five years her senior), he's had three bereavements since we were married, and I'm sure you'd have pitied him! He seemed so lost, we (*we* meaning the other wives!) scarcely knew how to comfort him. He had lost one wife just before I married him. She left four children, and I thought I never could love children of my own more. But, dear me, I found there was quite a new love for *them* when they came. I brought up my own little brothers and sisters, too, for mother died when I was thirteen, and left them to me, baby and all; and *I do* love children so dearly. But when my own, *own* first baby was laid in my arms, I just laughed with pleasure, — it was such a strange, sweet feeling. Of course that is something different, — a feeling, *if it is love, is one that you can't help, and deserve no credit for having.*

"He" (her Mr. D.) "has a wife now who is childless, and she is so fond of my present baby (my ninth, he is) that he loves her as much as he does me; all the difference is, he calls me mamma, and her Katie. She says her feeling is the same as if he were her own, but I say she only hasn't experienced the other, I have left him with her since morning."

This is but one instance of many where I found women fostering the children of their husband's other wives; but it was only at the Steerforths that I was an inmate of the household long enough to see, as I said, the unconscious tokens of a tender intimacy between the wives themselves,

Chicken Creek - The Sevier

We parted from our friends at Nephi with unfeigned regret. By six o'clock, of a frosty, starlight morning, we T.'s were roaming about the garden, punctual to the hour appointed for starting, — our valises packed, breakfast and family prayers long over. But we did not leave for two good hours. Some one or other in so large a party was sure to be unpunctual, and for our mutual safety it was necessary to travel in company, and, therefore, we always waited for the laggards.

During the early part of our drive there was little to interest us. On one side of the carriage we had the window drawn up, and the sun had not acquired power enough to thaw the rime off the glass; on the other, the plain spread out as on the last afternoon's journey, —

"Wild and bare,
Wide, wild, and open to the air,
Which had built up everywhere
An under-roof of doleful gray."

There were no more teams for the Nevada mines in sight. Far ahead of us a light cloud of dust indicated President Young's carriage, seen across the desert like the smoke of a steamer at sea. A horseman rode back to bid us close up, for the other carriages toiled equally far behind us in the heavy sand. The children began to tire of the journey before it was fairly begun. As for me, I picked up a book that some one had thrust into the carriage as we were quitting Nephi. It was gayly bound, printed in worn type, on coarse paper, much thumbed, and was entitled:

"Brigham Young's Destroying Angel. Being the Life, Confessions, and Startling Disclosures of the Notorious Bill Hickman. Written by Himself."

In the veracious pages of this work, I read that my gentle-looking host at Nephi had united with Mr. Hickman in murdering a party of six men. He had been particularly aided, too, by a demure gentleman who had pressed us to dine with him the preceding day; and whose wife's savory fried chicken had been highly extolled by those of our party who had accepted his hospitality. Mr. Hickman avers that they sank the bodies of two of their victims, with stones tied to their feet, in one of those "bottomless springs" we had noticed before coming to Nephi. And our halt at the Sevier crossing this day was to be made at the spot where two others were killed! Mr. Hickman's account is circumstantial, and he does not avoid blackening himself in the effort to criminate others. It is a curious commentary on the sanguinary character of the Mormons, as described by him, that he is living among them still. He was at Nephi only a few days before us.

It was a singular experience to read Hickman's book in the company of the man whom it was written to accuse of being the head of a band of Thugs, — a man who was at that very time under bail for a heavier amount than was exacted of Jeff Davis!

A cry of delight from the children caused me to look up. We had come to Chicken Creek, where there was a large pool, fed by springs. The stream rushing out from it cut its way round the side of a hill, leaping down several feet between banks fringed with long stalactites of ice. The sun pierced through the clouds and sparkled on the water; little Mabel and my boys, leaving the carriages, rushed over the hilly ridge, wild with delight. We took the opportunity, one and all, to warm ourselves by a stroll, while the horses were being watered.

Chicken Creek figures as the scene of a great Danite massacre. I expected the subject would be alluded to on our walk, but it was not.

Then we began to climb the ascent which separates the Juab from the Sevier Valley, and from the summit looked back over the now sunlit plain, with Nebo still towering over all the other mountains on the horizon. Then, down one long, slow descent after another, we came to the Sevier River and halted at the crossing. The Sevier has no outlet; it sinks in the sands of the desert, not very far to the west of where we were. To the eastward it flows through the San Pete country, where the Mormons, under Joseph A. Young, are organizing new settlements.

There being no facilities for irrigation, the Mormons have made no settlement at the Sevier crossing, although there is what the children called "a cunning little plain" there, which, by the way, is yearly overflowed. A few huts, partly burrowed into the hillside, and a shanty for the augmentation of the United States revenues, in front of which some Pioche teams had halted for refreshment, were planted on the farther side of the stream. Our horses were unharnessed to rest and feed, and I rambled about with my boys.

Although I did not believe one word of Hickman's accusations, I felt myself color with a feeling that I wronged the kind people about me when I caught myself instinctively glancing at the bushes that fringed the bank for the place where Hickman had said the victims tried to hide themselves; and at the swift river, into which, he said, the murderers threw three of them. Then I returned to my carriage, and shared in the bountiful lunch provided for us by the Mistresses Steerforth, forgetful of Mr. Hickman and his accusations of their goodman.

After dinner we toiled on steadily until darkness set in, with no other adventure than that of seeing the four horses of a great Pioche wagon take fright, and dashing along the rocky road, just missing President Young's carriage, rush aside into a cañon, down which we could hear them crashing on the rocks. We had seen enough of our friend "Lo," to know who would be the wreckers of that broken cargo.

It was dark when we reached our halting-place for the night.

Scipio

Round Valley, or Scipio, is the poorest and newest of the settlements we stopped at, and has been much troubled with the Indians. The Mormons say "troubled with Indians," as we might say "troubled with mosquitoes." No one had been killed for four years back, though cattle had been driven off that year, we were told.

The Bishop came riding out to meet us, a handsome, kindly-faced man, mounted on a horse that moved T.'s admiration. We were taken to the house of his second wife, a little, one-roomed log-cabin, with a lean-to behind, in which the cooking was done. The living-room was given up to us. Its main glory consisted in a wide chimney-place, on whose hearth a fire of great pine logs blazed, that sent a ruddy glow over the whitewashed logs of the wall and the canvas ceiling, and penetrated every corner of the room with delicious light and warmth. There was a substantial bedstead in one corner, and curtains of old-fashioned chintz were tacked from the ceiling around it as if it had been a four-poster, and a neat patchwork counterpane covered the soft feather-bed. A good rag-carpet was on the floor; clean white curtains hung at the windows; and clean white covers, edged with knitted lace, covered the various bracket-shelves that supported the housewife's Bible, Book of Mormon, work-basket, looking-glass, and a few simple ornaments. Two or three pretty good colored prints hung on the walls. Then there was a mahogany bureau, a washstand, a rocking-chair, and half a dozen wooden ones, with a large chest on which the owner's name was painted (oddly enough it was the same as that of the notorious "blonde" leader of a shameless troupe).

The small, round table was already spread for our supper with cakes, preserves, and pies; and the fair Lydia was busily engaged in bringing in hot rolls, meat, tea, and other good things, while a miniature of herself, still fairer and rosier, about two years old, trotted beside her; now endeavoring to rearrange the table by upsetting plates, and now making shy overtures of friendship to my boys, with the assistance of a blue-ribboned yellow kitten.

After our tea was over, the husband-bishop came in from his other dwelling, and with wife and baby withdrew to "go to meeting," leaving us in sole possession of the house. We heard no sound of their re-entering till morning, when our host came in to rouse up the smouldering fire.

I have given this minute description of the furniture of the mansion of which I was housekeeper for twelve hours, because it was a fair specimen of many of the humbler homes I visited in Utah. I have already remarked upon their unusual cleanliness, and have now only to note the absence of the colored prints of "Polly," "Nourmahal," etc., in "half-dress," common elsewhere.

The next time I visited Scipio was just at the breaking-up of winter. Snow lay deep on the heights and in the narrow canons, and Round Valley was an almost impassable quagmire of half-frozen mud. Again and again the horses stopped and stood with drooping heads, and an air that said, "I really have taken the last step I can make. Now I'm going to lie down;" and again and again they were coaxed forward at a slower than funeral pace, before we finally halted in front of Bishop Thompson's.

Our pretty hostess, "Aunt Lydia," was sick; a little girl said, opening the gate into the enclosure in which both houses stood, "and Mother expected us this time,"

The door was opened to admit us, by a slender, elegantly-dressed young lady.

"Mrs. Thompson?" I inquired, hesitatingly.

"No," she answered, smiling and blushing, "I am only a guest like yourself, Mrs. Thompson will be here in a moment: Sister Lydia is sick, and Mrs. Thompson thought some biscuits she had been baking would tempt her appetite, so she has run across with them. Here she is!"

"Sister Loraina Thompson" looked like an elder sister of Mrs. Lydia's, but was no relation. She had a large family of children, but seemed not in the least disconcerted by the addition to her household of our fellow-guest, her husband and baby, although she had to entertain Mr. Staines and young Kimball also; and to care for the invalid next door.

My husband now entered with Mr. Joseph A. Young and his brother Mahonri, who had joined us the day before; and taking a wee baby from the arms of the lady who had opened the door, and whom he introduced as his wife, Mr. Young presented the infant to T. as his namesake.

They had come across from the San Pete country to see us, and the baby was taking its first journey in the open air. It was a bright lively little thing, and lay on my knee basking in the warmth of the fire as the elders sat talking in one room, while Mrs. Thompson prepared supper in the other. She had a young girl to help her, but more than all, she had "faculty," and her meals were served with as much heat in them and coolness in herself, as if she had not both her rooms filled with guests and children.

When I recollected how many bowls and pans and plates I use when I try to make cake, and what a mess of sticky things I leave the cook to clear away, I could not but express my wonder at her deft ways. She came in after her tea-things were washed up, and sat beside me with her knitting. She laughed when I praised her, saying that it was no wonder — she had "had a girl to help her these three weeks" — but she never found the children in her way; they were a help. And so they were, the little eldest unrobing the younger ones for bed, or waiting at table without needing directions. They were well-trained, as well as healthy rosy children, and a little creature, who could scarcely speak plainly, sat on my knee, and carolled like a lark, "Up in the morning early," and "Put me in my little bed;" a still younger baby nodding an accompaniment with quite a good notion of the measure.

This Mrs. Thompson had grown up in the Mormon faith, our friend P. told me. Her mother died during the exodus, and she, then a mere child, had taken care of her younger brothers and sisters, and managed her father's house — "wagon-hold," I suppose one should call it — without aid from any one. Indeed, she continued to be her father's right hand until her marriage. Perhaps the rigorous training of circumstances in her youth made her consider what I thought such hard work, easy when it was done in her own home, working for her own children and her pleasant-faced husband.

Ought I to despise that woman? She certainly came up to Solomon's ideal of a virtuous wife. You would have despised her less, if you had felt the difference between her household and that of another woman at whose stronghold of freedom I halted the day afterwards. Above her house was exalted a pole bearing a candlebox lid, on which was painted,

"Old Boor
-bun. Segars."

Upon the roof lay old boots and shoes reluctant to be reduced to the rank of fertilizers, but giving token of what was to be seen inside. Entering the cabin, I found that the dirt-begrimed window prevented the household from needing a curtain, and the smoke-blackened logs of wall and ceiling were in keeping with the unmade bed and its tattered hangings. There was a very pretty baby here, too, which lay in its cradle and looked at me in silent wonder. The mother did no more. She never offered me a seat, nor the draught of water I had to ask for, and help myself to; merely remarking that she "hadn't no kind of a place for folks to come into. Her girl had left the place three weeks ago, and *she* warn't going to stay among the Mormons, if she could get her husband to quit, and go among Christian folks,"

She supposed, of course, that she was rude to a Mormon woman in me, and I confess that I did not claim her as a Christian sister.

Of course it would be as unfair to select such a wife as a specimen of "Gentile" pioneer females, as the energetic and active Mrs. Thompson of the average of Mormon women. Ill-health or Indolence and cheerful activity, are peculiar to neither orthodoxy nor heterodoxy. But a religious faith that animates the whole being, enabling a woman to be cheerful in spite of adverse circumstances, industrious in spite of sickness, loving God and her neighbor; and showing it by charity in word and deed; this faith above doctrine I have found quite as often among Mormon as among other Christian women.

We parted with Mrs. Young at the crossing of the river the morning after, and as we looked back upon the group just setting out over the snowy plain for their remote settlement, I felt profoundly sad. The refined-looking young creature, with her baby clasped in her arms, seemed no less proud of it than her husband was of her. Yet it seemed a desolate prospect for her to journey over that lonely country to a rough new settlement among the savages. Her ladylike manner and quiet tones made the life before her seem doubly incongruous. Poor child, she has had to take her part in life decidedly, too, and is isolated from her people and kindred in more than mere geographical distance. Her father and mother have left the church and Utah, and are among the most eloquent antagonists of Mormonism, while she clings to the faith they taught her in her childhood.

She seemed entirely contented, and praised her new home as much as if it lay in our green forest land, instead of among the dreary valleys of Utah. T. reminded me that our valleys, too, were snow-covered at this season, and that the plains of which she spoke would soon be a grassy sea, abounding in beautiful flowers. But what can atone for the absence of trees in a landscape?

Cedar Springs - Fillmore

When we emerged from Round Valley, before descending into the Pahvant country, we looked back upon a grand view. The nearer mountains were destitute of snow, and black and frowning; but on the far. horizon the sun lit up a number of snowy summits. Mount Nebo, still visible, highest of all, and most beautiful. Here and there were silvery threads of the Sevier passing to its mysterious grave in the desert.

Then we came to Cedar Springs, a place on the "Bench," looking out over a plain; near us, grassy enough to be entitled to be called ranch-ground, but wasting away into the Sevier Desert pure and simple. The little settlement itself was buried in fruit-trees.

Our day's journey carried us to Fillmore, the county seat of Millard. Both names were tributes of gratitude from the Mormons to a man who treated them fairly when they risked being "improved off the face of creation." They had then neither silver nor gold, nor shares in railroads or other corporations to "tip" him with; but in those days American statesmen were not all in the market, and the benefits they conferred were sometimes given without an extended palm. Millard Fillmore's town and county represent no *money* value to him, but the recorded thankfulness of a people should be worth something to the man, as the days draw near in which he must reckon up his deeds as they will appear in the light of heavenly wisdom.

From Cedar Springs we had an escort of citizens, on horseback, all the way to Fillmore; and from this time I often noticed that we took a mounted company from the night's halting-place, until we met other horsemen coming out to meet us from the next one.

An abrupt descent, into and out of the bed of Chalk Creek, brought us to Fillmore.

I ought to have been impressed by Fillmore, formerly the territorial capital; I ought to have been reminded of the fact by the big, "red, granite" building we passed where the territorial legislature used to assemble; I ought to have some idea of the size and population of the town; its schools, manufactures, and trading facilities.

Honestly, this is all I remember:

The place was on a rising ground above the plain, and was backed by peaked mountains. I remember that I was shown the great, red building as we passed it; I remember driving through an orchard that clothed two hillsides, sloping to a rivulet, with three neat cottages embowered among the trees, the homes of Bishop Collister. I noticed two cockney-looking villas in process of erection; having each its tower, bay-window, bow-window, dormer-window, balcony-verandah, recessed-porch, and pseudo-Gothic roof: features enough to jade the eye without allowing it to rest upon a yard of unbroken surface. I remarked the contrast to the house opposite where we halted, whose windows were à fleur de tête, and whose eaves projected scarcely six inches beyond the dull, unpointed brick walls; the only attempt at ornament being given by the impossible landscapes on the painted window-shades. Some Indians lounged against the fence, kicking up the dust lazily.

I am ashamed to confess that I remember no more of the external appearance of Fillmore; and there exists no "Murray" for Utah to make up travelers' memories for them.

The mistress of the mansion showed herself in the door-way; a large, loosely-built matron, "standing with reluctant feet" on the uninteresting border-land between middle and old age.

She rather made way for us to enter, than entreated us. We found her parlor in keeping with the exterior of the house, and heated almost to suffocation by a large sheet-iron stove. She sat with us a few moments, lamenting that her children were all married and gone; lamenting the trouble of housekeeping unaided; and by inference lamenting the trouble of entertaining me. I condoled with her most sincerely, regretting her latest trouble perhaps even more than she did.

After she withdrew to prepare our meal, a son of hers came in to call on T. This gentleman had frequently acted as sub Indian agent, and a quintette of Indians, emboldened by his presence, followed him into the room. When Mrs. Q. called us to supper, these gentry rose to accompany us. I looked helplessly at her. She said a few words in their dialect, which made them at once squat down again, huddling their blankets round them, with a pleasanter look on their dark faces than they had yet worn.

"What did your mother say to those men, Mr. O.?" I asked, curiously.

"She said 'These strangers came first, and I have only cooked enough for them; but your meal is on the fire cooking now, and I will call you as soon as it is ready.'"

"Will she really do that, or just give them scraps at the kitchen-door?" I pursued, thinking of "cold-victual" beggars at home.

"*Our* Pah-vants know how to behave," he answered, with the pride of a Kirkbride in his own lunatics. "Mother will serve them just as she does you, and give them a place at her table."

And so she did. I saw her placing clean plates, knives, and forks for them, and waiting behind their chairs, while they ate with perfect propriety. She rose a hundred per cent, in my opinion.

After supper, Kanosh, chief of the Pah-vant Indians, into whose country we had now entered, came to pay a formal visit to T. with the chiefs of his band.

There was something prepossessing in the appearance of Kanosh and his younger brother Hang-a-tah, but I cannot say as much for their friends. Kanosh has bright penetrating eyes, and a pleasant countenance. He cultivates a white moustache, and carries himself with a soldierly bearing. He wore a dark-blue uniform coat with bright buttons, yellow buckskin leggings, and moccasins, and had a black carriage-blanket thrown over one shoulder.

Hang-a-tah (the Red Blanket), a handsome, aquiline-nosed Indian, sat half-asleep on a chair near the stove, and coughed dismally from time to time a plaintive accompaniment to Kanosh's account of the decay of his band. Of Kanosh's own family he is the last. Brothers and children, he counted them up on his fingers; "all gone, all sick, no *shoot*, die *sick*."

Most of Kanosh's court squatted on the floor; but of those who occupied chairs, two attracted my notice by their entire want of interest in the proceedings and their intense unflagging interest in themselves.

One evidently felt himself to be an exquisite. This fellow kept stretching his legs and admiring each alternately, yawning to show his white teeth, affecting to go to sleep and awake with a start — all in order to attract the attention of the white squaws. The other who sat next the beau, a very ugly young warrior, regarded him with silent contempt, confident in the superior attractiveness of his own person. This one's role I perceived to be that of the cynic. He did not glance towards us once, until just as he was leaving. Then he loftily passed us in review with the air of a Sim. Tappertit. The next instant, however, his eye was caught by his own image in the glass. He advanced to it at once with undissembled admiration, and stood posturing before it, and adjusting a strip of leather, dotted with tin studs, that covered the parting of his coarse, black locks, until the rest of the party had filed out.

Kanosh, an old acquaintance of 1858, mourned to my husband over the changes death had caused in his band since then, and asked to be told the truth: were *any* gifts or annuities allotted him by the government; or was he cheated out of them by the agents; had he not a right to stay on the farm his band cultivated at Corn Creek; why must he "be poked off with guns to Uintah?"

I do not intend to report Kanosh's set speech, although it struck me as decidedly clever. His prejudice against Mr. Dodge, the agent, has probably no greater foundation than most Indian complaints. How great that is, I reserve my opinion! My husband made Kanosh dictate a statement in his own words, which I took down in my pocket-diary. The astute old fox made three persons read it to him to make sure I was not cheating him, before he made his X mark:

"One snow-time since, I got blankets; no flour, no beef, but a little last spring; no flour, no oats, no wheat, no corn, no bullets; no see nothing but Dodge; [1] Dodge talk heap talk; weino pesharrony katz yak — good talk, but no give."

KANOSH, his **X** mark,

Fillmore, Dec. 17, 1872.

I stayed at one of Bishop Collister's cottages in the orchard the next time I visited Fillmore.

The Mormons say that frost after frost killed the peach-trees and cut the apple-trees to the ground when they first made a settlement in the place, and did so year after year. Any reasonable people would have given up trying to produce fruit; but the Mormons are quite *un*reasonable in matters of faith, and some brother or sister had had it revealed, or had a vision, or "felt to prophesy" that it would yet be noted among the towns of Utah for its fruits. They persevered, and so I know what perfectly delicious apples they now harvest. Our bedroom at Fillmore had a great basket full of them, golden and rosy, sweet and tart, pippins and Spitzenbergs; with which we amused our palates between meals, and filled every nook in the carriage next day.

My new hostess was, I believe, a daughter of my first one. What a pretty creature she was! Tall and graceful; with the loveliest of dark eyes! And she had three sweet little children — "three left out of seven." Her husband had lost eleven out of his twenty-eight children. Wife Mary had borne him seven, Caroline twelve, and Helen nine.

These numbers are not unusual in Utah, nor were they among the Puritans, our ancestors. But their *past* experience, at all events, gives the Mormons no right to claim that the mothers of families rear a greater number proportionately than with us. More children may have been born to each mother; but in each new settlement in Utah, the first stirring of the soil, the chemical exhalations, the fierce, shadeless heats of summer, caused many deaths. "Then was there a voice heard in Ramah, Rachel mourning for her children refused to be comforted because they were not." Much as it has improved of late years in salubrity, I am far from sure that Utah is yet a very healthy land for children. But as far as my experience goes, I think they are very kindly, as well as carefully nurtured. They are admitted very freely to their parents' society, and are not always "snubbed" when they proffer their small contributions to the conversation going on among their elders. Generally, too, they are well-behaved. I think the tie between mother and children is closer than that between them and the father. Whether the fathers can love each one of so many children, as much as they could if there were six or seven — or *say fifteen* — less, I will not pretend to say.

I have seen a Mormon father pet and humor a spoiled *thirty-fifth* child (a red-headed one, too!) with as unreasonable fondness as the youngest papa could show his first-born.

Two of the children my hostess at Fillmore had lost were twin girls, and she lamented over "Ada and Ida" quite as much as if they might not have grown up to be thirteenth or fourteenth wives to somebody. It had been one of the accepted beliefs with which my mind was stocked before entering Utah, that every mother would be found to regret the birth of a daughter as a misfortune. This is not so. They honestly believe in the grand calling their theology assigns to women; "that of endowing souls with tabernacles that they may accept redemption." Nowhere is the "*sphere*" of women, according to the gospel of Sarah Ellis, more fully recognized than in Utah; nowhere her "*mission*" according to Susan Anthony, more abhorred.

And yet they vote? True; but they do not take more interest in general politics than you do. If your husband, Charlotte, your father, brothers, and all the clergymen you know approved of your voting, it would not strike you as an unfeminine proceeding. And if the matter on which your vote was required was one which might decide the question whether you were your husband's wife, and your children legitimate, you would be apt to entertain a determined opinion on the subject.

Nobody thought us unfeminine for being absorbingly interested in our national affairs during the war. The Utah women take a similar interest in the business of the world outside that concerns *them;* and pray over congressional debates as we prayed for our armies.

[1] Mr. D. is said to have been a Baptist clergyman or missionary.

Cove Creek Fort

From Fillmore we climbed to Cove Creek Fort, a forty-eight miles' drive. About twelve miles out of Fillmore we reached Corn Creek, which we crossed at a small Mormon village, near what Kanosh pompously called *his city*. The Pah-vants are settled on a farm by government treaty.

I looked with great interest at the surrounding mountains, as being the old haunts of Wah-ker; and the narrow canon was pointed out to me which was his burial-place.

Kanosh had invited us to visit his city, but it lay out of the direct road, and the length of our day's journey permitted no excursions. Kanosh Is a Mormon convert, and prides himself on his "white ways." His favorite wife — an Indian girl, brought up in a Mormon family — persuaded him to let her keep house "Mormone fashion" for him. The Mormons had built her a nice little cottage, where she had real doors and windows, six chairs ranged round the room, a high-post bedstead in the corner, and plates and dishes in a press. She had her cows, — and made butter, — her poultry, eggs, and vegetables; and in her day Kanosh proudly displayed a stiff clean shirt-front and high collar every Sunday.

Naturally, the other squaws were jealous. Kanosh went hunting, and on his return, three weeks afterwards, the poor young wife had disappeared. Kanosh was sure that his eldest squaw had murdered her. What did he do? He told her that God had seen her do it; and bade her die. And she gradually faded away; and in less than a year she died, confessing that she had taken her victim by the hair as she knelt among the plants in her garden, pulled back her head, and cut her throat. Then she had dragged the body away, and buried it in the cornfield.

After the Christian wife's murder, Kanosh mourned in a sincere way that deeply gratified his Mormon friends. But he and the remaining squaws couldn't manage his affairs in her fashion. He wore his shirts, however, faithfully and honorably, till the buttons, the sleeves, and collars all deserted him. As to the poultry, when the eggs had accumulated to three bushels, or thereabouts, his band made a grand feast, and, Indian-like, ate up all the chickens, — literally all except the feathers, — and all the eggs, good and bad.

The house Kanosh still uses on grand occasions, as the queen uses Buckingham Palace when she holds a drawing-room. To gratify him, Brigham Young paid him a visit there. The president was on one of his journeys south, and stopped in his carriage before the door. No notice was taken of his arrival, and when he sent a rider in to announce him, expecting Kanosh to come out, Kanosh sent answer, that when he went to see "Bigham, Bigham sat still in his house; and what was manners for Bigham, was manners for Kanosh." "He's right," said Brigham, and, leaving the carriage, he went in to pay his respects to the chief.

Kanosh was perched on the high four-posted bed, sitting cross-legged "plump in the feathers." He wore a heavy, pilot cloth great-coat, buttoned to the chin, a pair of new cowhide boots, and his finest red blanket over all. It was a very warm day in May, and the window was closed. The perspiration streamed down his face, but he sat erect and motionless, feeling that he "must do something for dignity." President Young tried hard to maintain his gravity, but it was completely upset when the valance of the bed was cautiously lifted at one side, and the youngest wife protruded her head, and looked up to survey the general effect of her lord's appearance.

We could not see the Kanosh mansion from the road, and after leaving Corn Creek, I do not remember passing any settlement that day. I suppose the country had too little water, for I remember that we carried water from Corn Creek for the horses, to the sheltered little hollow in the hills where we "nooned." I know our bottle of milk was frozen solid, and we had to depend on the charity of our neighbors. The Mormons all quaffed, with great apparent relish, a horrible beverage called "composition," made of ginger, cayenne-pepper, cloves, and bay berries ground to powder, sweetened, and mixed with cream, diluted with boiling water. This stuff had not frozen, and they drank it cold.

The day itself was so cold that our picnic was eaten in our closed carriages, instead of in the usual social open-air fashion.

The sun was sinking when we reached Cove Creek Fort, and drove in under its archway. T. soon called me outside to look at the landscape, and see how lonely a place we were in. The fort lay in a volcanic basin, geologically esteemed to be the crater of an extinct volcano. All round it were oddly-peaked, ragged-looking mountains glowing in purple and gold, looking no more substantial than the cloud-mountains of sunset with which they mingled. Farther on the road we were to travel next day some wagons were encamped, their supper -fires already kindled. At the foot of a hill hard by, a solitary thread of smoke beside a single "wick-i-up," as the Utes call their lodges, showed where a young Indian lay who had shot himself while hunting the day before. Round the fort were fields with unusually strong and high fences; outside it on the north was a very large barn with a well-filled yard, surrounded by a stockade. Our teams were being led in, to the discomposure of some cows who had a proprietary air as they moved sulkily aside to let the intruders enter. The smoke of their warm breath made a cloud in the frosty air.

There was a broad sheet of ice to cross before entering the fort, and I wondered whence the water came, as I saw no water-course near. The fort has gray stone walls about thirty feet high, adorned with tall chimneys north and south, and with two great gateways opening east and west. Over one is inscribed

"Cove Creek Fort Ranche,
1867."

Entering the large paved courtyard, we found it filled with our vehicles. Six doors opened to the north and as many to the south, giving admission to large and lofty rooms. I was not sorry to see a magnificent pitch-pine fire blazing on the hearth in mine, for the fort is — 6000? — I forget how many ungenial feet above tide, and the night was very cold. Our room was nicely furnished, and looked very cozy as we drew our chairs around the centre-table, which had a number of well-chosen books upon it. The children were pleased to recognize another of the pretty pink-fringed, linen table-covers of which so many had already greeted us on our journey, and wondered whether the "Co-op" had bought a large invoice from Claflin, that we found them thus broadcast through the territory. It made us feel New York quite near us.

We were called to supper on the other side of the fort, feeling our way over the icy ground, guided by a stream of light from the open door of a guard-room, where stacks of arms were piled, and a group of stout fellows sat before a blazing fire.

We supped in the telegraph office, where the ticking of the instrument insisted on being heard as we all knelt down for prayers. — Prayers after the patriarchal Hebrew manner; a shot-proof fort; an electric battery clicking the latest New York news; armed men; unarmed women with little children; a meal served with dainty precision in a refectory walled with rough-hewn stone: this medley of antichronisms is Mormon all over.

Here, too, was this fort, designed to serve the same purpose, in the saints' eyes, as the interpreter's house of the Pilgrim's Progress. Both were built "for the entertainment and comfort of pilgrims, and their protection against ill-favored ones." And surely Bunyan never dreamed of more devilishly ugly Apollyons than the red warriors of Utah.

Although it stands in the friendly Pah-vant country, the fort commands a pass on the old Spanish trail from California to New Mexico, used still by the Navajoes, whose raids give the Mormons much trouble and anxiety.

Our dinner-supper was excellent, but neither "wave-breast" nor "heave-shoulder" decked the board. Stewed chickens, clarified apples, and cream furnished no texts for "profitable discourse" from our entertainers, thou eh I marveled at the presence of such dainties in that inhospitable-looking spot.

I saw but one woman in the fort, and she had a group of children hanging to her skirts. I thought she must have had her hands full to provide bread and meat enough for her hungry guests. The shining cleanliness of the table-linen and glass was worthy of a Quakeress, when she has "given her mind to it," yet I found that every drop of water had to be "packed;" *i.e.* carried a mile and a half. Cove Creek is led into the fort in summer — though its supply cannot be depended upon, as it frequently dries up. But in winter they have to turn its waters back to their natural channel, as it "overflows the fort with ice" — a result which had just followed an attempt to let it on in our honor. Two wells had been dug, each one hundred feet deep, but without striking water. It seemed to me a foolish thing to build a fort where a besieged garrison would suffer so much from want of water. But I was answered, when I hinted this, that the fort was only meant to defend travelers and the family of the ranche against Indian forays. It was too far from any settlement for a single family to be safe in the open country, and there was too little water for irrigation to warrant the placing of a settlement. I was reminded, when I called it a dreary region, that we were now in the depth of winter, and that the magnificent haystacks I had seen were the produce of the ranche. They said, indeed, that the soil was the richest in the world when irrigated. I think, however, they admitted that the climate was too Arctic for the apple-tree, and where that cannot flourish, is, I respectfully adhere to my opinion, no Garden of Eden.

The great Mormon crop — of children — thrives at Cove Creek Ranche, however. As we left the table, we noticed a little two-year-old girl, whom I shall always maintain to be the loveliest baby ever seen. The diminutive beauty accepted the compliments of the party in a manner that showed she was used to them. One remarked her rosy cheek, clear blue eye, and golden hair; another her white skin; another her tiny foot and ankle, and the plump little leg that rose above her white sock.

"This is the child you administered to. Brother Brigham," said the gratified mother.

President Young had not been listening, but seeing that he was appealed to, answered, "Oh! ahem? ay!" first interjectionally, then interrogatively, and then affirmatively — which appeared to be entirely satisfactory; for she went on:

"Yes, you laid hands on her when she was only six days old, and she seemed as if she had not an hour to live."

This was not the first time I had heard the Mormons allude to the laying-on of hands. It was explained to be their revival of the early Christian custom enjoined by the Apostle James:

"Is any sick among you? Let him call for the elders of the church; and let them pray over him, anointing him with oil in the name of the Lord: and the prayer of faith shall save the sick, and the Lord shall raise him up."

As we crossed the court on our way back to our rooms, I remarked to a lady near me, "Mrs. Lucy, the orthodox Christian churches no longer practice the custom (for the Roman Catholic anointing of the dying is a different one), because the days of miracles are over."

"Ah," she replied; "the orthodox churches, as you call them, Mrs. T., only assert *that,* because their faith is so torpid that they cannot be blessed with miracles. As our Saviour said, they cannot do many mighty works *because of their unbelief;* and again, the word preached does not profit them, not being mixed with *faith* in them that hear it. You Presbyterians," she continued, "reject the traditions of the Church and the authority of the early fathers, and rely upon what the Bible says. Now, James's epistle is one of the very last printed in the New Testament. Where is your authority for considering his injunction to have been abrogated subsequently? Don't you see it is a salve to your consciences which you apply, because your faith is so weak that you prefer to trust your sick to the different human systems of doctoring rather than to the hands of God?"

What did I answer? Oh, I said, loftily, that T. did not wish me to enter into theological arguments. I found this always a very safe reply; my Mormon friends thoroughly approving the teaching of St. Paul, that a woman should refer all theological puzzles to her own husband at home. Ah, St. Paul, little didst thou foresee how busy our husbands would be all day in Wall Street, how tired and cross every evening at home! Fancy our asking *them* to extract roots of doctrine for us!

Darkness had fallen by the time supper was over; but the great gates were left open later than usual, as one of our baggage wagons had not yet come up. T. took the little boys to see the wounded Indian. The squaws had bitten the flesh around the wound to stop the bleeding, and had then erected the wick-i-up over him as he lay, being afraid to let him be carried as far as the friendly shelter of the fort.

I went to sit for half an hour with the ladies of our party, and groping my way back in the darkness came suddenly on the two squaws, who had raised the sash of my window a little, and were so absorbed in peeping into the lighted splendors of the apartment, having lifted a corner of the blind to do so, that they did not hear my approach. It would be hard to say whether I or they were most startled. They contrived by signs and repetitions of "Bigham's" name to let me know they wanted to see him, so I conducted them to where his family were still seated round the fire, and then slipped away, leaving them to dispose of their visitors as they liked.

I found the chatelaine giving a few final touches to the comfort of my room, when I returned, and falling into conversation with her about the loneliness of her position, her answer was that she was seldom alone, but that, as it happened, Mr. H. had been obliged to take his other wife to Salt Lake City for her health, and that the opportunity had been taken to send "their" elder children there to school for the winter, while they could enjoy the benefit of maternal supervision. The night was stinging cold; but we did not rise next day till the fires were blazing. The chimneys of Cove Creek Fort, I can attest, draw superbly; and the early cup of hot coffee, I found most of our party willing to admit, was more cheering to the spirit than "composition" cold.

When we set out the sun was fully up, though it seemed to give no warmth; the sky was intensely blue, the air blue too, and sparkling with ice dust. The horses' hoofs rang merrily on the iron-bound ground. Looking back on the fort, I watched the U. S. flag waving us farewell, until it was no larger than a carnation flower, — the loveliest possible bit of color to my homesick eyes.

I noticed in the daylight that the walls of the fort were composed of dark blocks of lava, and only reduced to a grayish tone by the whiteness of the mortar cementing the courses of masonry.

Prairie Dog Hollow - Indian Creek

Our day's journey was but twenty-four miles, and lay through what might by courtesy be called a wooded country. At the summit of each little pass we found ourselves in a thicket of cedars, so ragged and forlorn, and so evidently small for their age, that they looked as if a forest had been set out on the plain and buried to the neck in drifting sand. The road was rough, for the sand but partially concealed the ledges of volcanic rock we were crossing — "rocks full of bubbles," as the children called them.

We were now not far east of the Nevada mining district, and a halt was made on one of the summits to let us see "where we were," while the tired horses took breath. On our left a great ragged snow-streaked mountain was pointed out as "Baldy," at whose foot lay the Bullionville gold-mining region. On the right, among a range of gravel mountains, rose up one all cliffs and precipices "serrated deeply, five-parted, conspicuous," as the manuals of botany have it; its top resembling the crater of a volcano, which it probably was. This mountain remained in sight all day, its hard features never undistinguishable from the softer profiles of its fellows. Below us lay the dusty plain, dotted far with white-topped wagons, bound for Pioche. Beyond, the horizon was crowded with range after range of mountains; and a depression in the most distant faint blue outline was pointed out as our goal — the pass of Kannarra.

At Kannarra we were to cross the rim of the basin, and descend at once into warmer lands. We had been crossing one minor basin after another since leaving Salt Lake, but all were contained in the trough of the great basin, walled in on the east by the Wahsatch range.

The great basin is itself elevated thousands of feet above tide, and the mountains that looked down upon us claimed a height of from ten to twelve thousand feet. No wonder that the summit where we stood was cold in that December weather, or that we looked longingly towards Kannarra's distant gateway. By this time we were half way from Salt Lake on our journey. Each day had seemed to grow colder and the wind to blow harder; and now and then snow squalls would come up and terrify us with their petty tornadoes.

Brilliantly as the sun shone upon us, we were glad to creep back into our carriages. Our way led down Wild Cat Cañ'on, a pass so narrow and winding that it is not surprising that the Mormons were long in finding it. It now affords them a natural easy descent into Prairie Dog Hollow. Formerly they let their wagons down here over the bluffs by ropes, the men and teams scrambling down as best they might.

I do not know why it was necessary to go down into Prairie Dog Hollow at all, like the king of France in the adage. I am sure there was nothing to see when we got there. A circular sweep of the hills surrounded the little glen, making it a delightfully warm and sheltered halting-place for our noonday rest. It was treeless, shrubless, and destitute of water, however;

and the dog-towns and ant-hills, with which its surface was plentifully besprinkled, showed no signs of life.

The little communist citizens were wrapped in their winter sleep, and the children could not elicit a remonstrant squeak as they ran among the tiny domes, accompanied by their friend, Elder Potteau. As for me, one of our company, a dark-eyed, rosy little Welshwoman, who had hitherto proceeded no further in making my acquaintance than to exchange morning and evening salutations, plucked up spirit enough — it could scarcely be owing to the inspiration of the cheering cup of composition — to join me in a ramble before the horses were put to.

Her husband, one of the kindest of T.'s old friends of '46, had been among the first to greet us on our arrival in Salt Lake City. In answer to T.'s inquiries after his good wife, he had produced her daguerreotype to show me. She had "passed behind the veil" two years before, but he spoke of her death with evident emotion.

"Here, at least," I had thought, "is one man, high in Mormon esteem, yet a monogamist."

It was a shock to me to recognize him on our journey, accompanied by this other wife, and I now learned from her that the fair-haired son who was with them was not her offspring, nor the offspring of "Helen," but that of a third wife. Yet again the third wife did not claim him, having "given him away," at his birth, to Helen. "For all of Helen's children had grown up by that time, and she brought Le Roy up as her own."

Mistress Jane told me that the youngster could not hear his adopted mother's death spoken of without weeping; and thereupon she wept herself as she eulogized "Sister Helen's" virtues. Helen was much older than the other two wives, and they looked up to her as a mother. She had taught their children entirely, being a well-educated lady. She was very neat and nice in her ways, although she wore homespun, like the rest of us. She regulated the family affairs, deciding even such little matters as whether Johnny should have his old boots cobbled, or wear his new ones.

The house was well-ordered in Helen's time; yet never so stirring, jocund, and cheerful.

Mrs. Jane spun and wove, and worked in the dairy cheerfully. "That's what I'm fit for," she said; "but Sister Helen knew how everything ought to be done; and she was so sweet-tempered that there never was any jealousy or quarreling in the family while she lived."

"Mrs. Jane" herself was a born worker, — never happier, as I afterwards found when I knew her better, than in helping others; and so fond of children, that she used to smuggle my boys away for a morning sometimes, always returning them with their hair elaborately curled. I used to wonder at this, but I found that she was "homesick for the children" left behind in Salt Lake City. "Her own children, of course?" you say.

By no means. "The bigger ones could manage very well without her; but she yearned for the little chaps," her own and the other wife's, who were missing her, too, she was sure. And when we returned to Salt Lake City, and she brought a flock of children to see me, the special pet who clung to her skirts, and who seemed to have had every hair of his head curled separately, was the third wife's child!

Jane had been one of the hand-cart pilgrims, and had pushed her cart, and done all the cooking for her father's family, sixteen in number, at every halt they made for two months. Like many of the younger women, she had not "experienced conviction" at the time when her elders joined the church, but had fallen into line because the rest did. Her convictions seemed certain now, and her reverence for her husband was unbounded. He was a simple, sincere, and upright old man, a real *patriarch,* for whom no one could entertain a disrespectful feeling. He joined us as we walked, and seemed pleased with the subject of our conversation.

Mrs. Helen, they told me, was a sincere Christian, a firm Presbyterian for more than six years after her husband changed his faith. After they were driven from Nauvoo the last time, the trials of the journey and encampments on the prairie softened her heart. Never a murmur crossed her lips, or as much as a word against the decrees of Providence; but her favorite text of Scripture, often repeated on the pilgrimage and in the early years of the settlement, till it grew to be remembered as the motto of her life, was, "All this way hath the Lord thy God led thee, to humble thee and prove thee, and to give thee peace in thy latter end."

Her husband only remembered one remark escaping her that looked like dissatisfaction with her lot. It was when they reached the promised land and looked down on the Salt Lake Valley. There were about six small cottonwood trees then in all the valley, and Helen looked at them a long time. Then said she to her husband, "Father, we have come fifteen hundred miles in wagons, and a thousand miles through the sage-brush; and

I'd get into the wagon tomorrow, and travel a thousand miles farther, to see shade-trees instead of these rocks and sands."

She was *so* fond of "growing things," her husband said, that she languished in health in the confinement for safety, and he petitioned the brethren to let him establish himself outside it, — on the hill where the Lion House now stands. It was thought a foolhardy thing to do. and objection was made; but with Helen's consent, he solemnly took the responsibility upon himself, and they placed their dwelling beside City Creek.

Helen had brought a whole bushel of fruit-tree kernels, and other seeds. "Now, mother," he told her, "I'll set every one of these out, and you'll soon have shade-trees enough."

Helen took the greatest pride in her little plantation. The trees were about a foot high, when the grasshoppers ate them down to the roots. They ate everything in the garden with entire impartiality.

Great was Helen's disappointment; but after a time many of her little trees threw up fresh shoots. Shortly after, too, one of the brethren, who had invested all his savings in the purchase and transportation of ten thousand young fruit-trees, divided the few dozen of choice varieties, which he had been able to save from the grasshoppers, among the families, and Helen secured some which she nursed and petted as in other days she had tended her roses and geraniums.

No one had money to repay the gardener for his treasures, but they gave him bullets, axes, flour, — very little of that, — nails; anything of which they could spare a part, and almost everybody bought a few.

I asked Mr. ___ whether they had ever been maltreated by the Indians in consequence of living outside the fort,

Helen was greatly affrighted once, he said, but that was all. He had made his dwelling as secure as he could with bolts and bars, and bought a heavy watch-dog. Indians often came to beg, but they behaved well, as he and the dog were always on the premises. One day, however, he was forced to go to the canon to be absent all day. Helen felt so timid that she called Tiger inside the house and shut him up in the bedroom.

Noonday came, and she had forgotten her terrors, when a malevolent-looking Indian came boldly into the kitchen. He had probably watched the house, and supposed the dog gone as well as the man. He asked for bread. She gave him some biscuit and four ounces of flour, — all she had to give, — but he threw it down and demanded more, working himself up on her refusal until he felt angry enough to take aim at her with his arrow. She sprang to the door of the bedroom, threw it open, crying, "Tige, take him!" The dog darted out and flew at the ruffian's throat.

The attack was so unexpected that the Indian went at once to the floor, and there man and beast rolled over and over in a desperate struggle. The dog conquered. The Indian cried like a child for mercy; and when she bade the dog quit him, threw his bow and quiver at her feet, and made signs imploring her pity for his wounds. She was horribly frightened, but she bade the dog watch him while she went for warm water and bathed the bites, and tore some of her scanty supply of linen into bandages.

He lay on her floor some time, and then crawled away, and was never again seen near the settlement.

Helen lived, said her husband, to see the lonely house surrounded by beautiful villas, each set like her own in an orchard of thriving trees, and at her feet a fast-growing city, with no other sign of danger threatening It than the presence on the height above it of the white buildings of Camp Douglas, under whose guns the city lies.

The gardener of whom Mr. ___ had spoken was my children's friend. Elder Potteau. I mentioned the subject of his fruit-tree investment to him when we gathered round the evening fire, asking him how he disposed of all his "payments in kind."

He assured me that all had proved useful.

"Nails!" Why, he had sorted the nails into separate kegs, till, by the time he was ready to build, he had almost enough for the house he began with.

Like all the Mormons of the first immigration, Elder P. spoke with deep feeling of the sufferings they endured when the crops, whose seed they had denied themselves bread to save, were devoured by the "army of grasshoppers sent to try their faith." All their feeble efforts to burn or drown or kill them failed before the presence of such vast numbers of the enemy. "The land was as a Garden of Eden before them, and a desolate wilderness behind them," he quoted, with rare appropriateness.

On a Sunday morning he walked sorrowfully among his dying fruit-trees, too heartsick to begin work again, but too much of a gardener to refrain altogether from using the hoe in his hand here and there. Elder John Taylor and two others came up, and said to him, —

"Potteau, we can do nothing ourselves; there is no use in our working without God's blessing. If he chooses to take pity on us, our crops may be saved. He has commanded us to keep holy the Sabbath day, and Brother Brigham says we had better all come to meeting and pray."

They did so. Then came the wind that brought the snow-white gulls, and they consumed the grasshoppers. The crops were saved, "and God," said he, "restored to us the years that the locust had eaten. And we know that He Is in the midst of Israel, and is the Lord our God, and none else; and His people shall never be ashamed." [1]

Why should not believers in special providences argue that the "keeping holy the Sabbath-day" prevented the gulls from being frightened away by human noises, and permitted them to do their work in peace?

[1] Joel ii. 27. This is a great chapter with the Mormons.

Beaver

I was quite sorry to part from Mrs. Jane, when the horses were once more put to. Short as our afternoon's drive was, it proved a tiresome one: we were obliged to move so slowly, and the children's usual chatter had to be hushed. I had given my husband's place in the carriage to a sick lady, and I feared that they might arouse the beautiful pale creature from a sleep into which she fell nearly as soon as the motion of the carriage began.

The barren hills and plains gave way to one scene that reminded us of home: I think it was "Indian Creek," where a shallow stream flowed between gently-rising banks fringed with cottonwood trees. There were nicely-fenced-in fields here, and a decent farmhouse, but the people were all away. There had been an Indian alarm, we were told, and the settlers had been warned in from exposed points. The children begged to stop a little longer to refresh their eyes with the sight of "running water, and trees big enough to look at," but after the horses had done drinking we had to pass on to arrive at Beaver before dusk.

We went on descending until we reached the hard gravelly plain in which Beaver lies. Some one told me that no mice existed there because the soil was too hard for them to work. But hard or not, the Mormons have picked out and fenced some three thousand [1] acres fit for cultivation.

Although I must say that the fields *I* saw looked as if the pebbly bed of some ancient stream had been fenced in! Moreover, it is *rather* frosty: last summer there were only seven weeks between the frosts. But Beaver will flourish, because it has an abundant supply of almost the only perfectly soft water in the territory.

We entered the town. Something reminded me of our own villages. Was it the unpainted clap-board shanties?

"No, mamma," cried Will, "they must be going to have a railroad built here. Look at the signs!" They were the signs which the child had noticed at every railroad station from Omaha to Ogden. There, were the familiar letters, SALOON; the red curtains behind windows reading without spelling, — Rum-Hole; and round the corner was BILLIARDS.

Our invalid companion had roused herself to greet a boy -brother who came galloping up to meet us, I asked her why there was this difference between Beaver and the other Mormon settlements, and she replied with her usual gentle brevity, and without the ghost of a smile, "There is an Army-Post here."

I intended to remark that I did not see the application of the reply, but Evy, with a flush of shame on his face, quietly pointed out to me the dear blue-coats that I would have been so glad to greet in this out-of-the-way place, — anywhere but on the backs of the tavern loungers, who gazed at the Mormon procession as our carriages went forward to Bishop Macbeth's house.

This gentleman's house was so large a one as to accommodate almost the whole of our party, but it was presided over only by his pretty daughter, — his still prettier wife being so great an invalid as to be unable to do more than make an appearance in her easy-chair enveloped in soft shawls for a short half-hour after supper. To spare her nerves, the roomy parlor adjoining her chamber was left unoccupied, and the dining-room was used as a sitting-room, while our meals were served in the kitchen, whose dainty cleanliness obviated all necessity for the excuses the young hostess made for leading the way there when we went to supper. She had several assistants in her housekeeping labors, and I supposed they were neighbors or servants. The tone of the household appeared so thoroughly monogamic, the illness of its female head so manifestly forming the chief topic of concern to husband and daughter, that it never occurred to me, until after I had left Beaver, to inquire whether Mr. Macbeth had more wives than one.

He had. Three.

So that my diary with its notes of satisfaction over finding myself "once more under a true wife's roof" reads rather absurdly.

Bishop Macbeth and his wife and daughter looked and talked like Virginians, F. F. V. Virginians, too; and he rode like a Virginian-born, which he was, — on a black horse that would have made President Grant envious. The pretty daughter in her gray dress, and purple cloth jacket braided with black, was as much of a little lady as any belle of the James or Rappahannock River plantations, and as much of a tart little copperhead, too! The majority of the American-born women I met In Utah were Northern in feeling.

Our party broke up soon after supper, most of its members going to meeting; but as I found that Miss Julia's hospitality had warmed the large bed-room set apart for me, and provided a plentiful supply of towels to relish the delicious soft water of Beaver, I preferred giving the children a thorough bathing before the brightly-blazing fire, and then writing the valuable notes I have referred to before seeking my own rest. In the morning I heard noises outside, and going to the window saw about twenty Indian warriors dismounting from their horses; the leader conferring with Bishop Macbeth, at whose order the gates of the tithing-yard were thrown open, and — shall I use the civilized phrase? — a Committee of savage citizens proceeded to demolish half a haystack, carrying out armfuls of hay, and throwing it down before the horses of the band, now picketed in front of the yard.

The summons to breakfast came, and the fair Julia was just leading us into the sight of an appetizingly-spread table. A woman (was she a stepmother?) was placing a pot of steaming coffee on it, and another woman (another stepmother?) was withdrawing a pan of hot rolls from the oven, when Miss Julia suddenly paused, and saying, "I beg your pardon; you will have to wait a few moments!" closed the door between us and herself. Not, however, before I had seen the outer door of the kitchen thrown open, and Bishop Macbeth enter, followed by the Indians, he saying to the women, "Now, good people, you'll have to satisfy these folks first."

Sitting hungrily beside the parlor window, I soon saw our copper-colored supplanters returning to their horses' company with their hands and mouths full of our good breakfast. Our hostesses seemed to have taken it as a matter of course, for in less than half an hour we were demolishing more hot rolls, coffee, chickens, and other good things, which were smilingly pressed upon us from an apparently inexhaustible larder.

The Indians had come, I suppose, to see President Young; but, if so, they were disappointed, for we started immediately after breakfast.

[1] My informant was a woman. She is not to be held responsible for accuracy within a thousand acres or so more or less.

Buckhorn Spring - Red Creek

The storm which had been following us so long threatened to envelop us all the forenoon; occasionally snow-flakes falling from the low clouds that had hidden the surrounding mountain-tops. A party of men from Beaver rode out some miles on the plain with us. Passing a group of horses, closely fenced in with wattles, we saw several Indians waiting for us, who approached President Young's carriage, but as he did not stop they dropped behind in silence. Their faces were painted up in their best style. One represented an overdone Neapolitan sunset, and another flamed in metallic yellows like a brazen idol. All wore showy Navajo blankets — an incidental proof of the truth of Kanosh's assertion that no blankets had been furnished them by the United States. These Indians were Pah-vants, the last we saw of Kanosh's band; and I presume the reason that President Young would not stop to hear their complaints, was the same that made him decline so cavalierly to receive Kanosh, at Fillmore; dislike to being supposed to be in league with disaffected Indians while government had him under its frown.

Three or four unarmed bands of Navajoes have been coming up as far as Beaver to trade this year. They want horses, and will not take money; and talk of intending to steal no more; but the Mormons think these virtuous professions are the result of one of their bishops on the Arizona frontier threatening to establish a fortified ranche at the Colorado ford which they must cross in returning from their raids on Utah.

The Mormons, as practical a people as they are daring, have gone to the expense of constructing a telegraph line down to the very limit of Utah Territory.

Look at Dore's "Wandering Jew," striding along through forest and desert, always lonely, and possessed of secret knowledge he cannot impart. The artist makes the long perspective of tree-tops simulate crosses to reproach Ahasuerus. The same weird effect is given by these poles, and that endless slender wire, stretching over sandy plain and volcano-blasted mountain. The telegraph is protected from the Indians only by their own superstition. They believe it is charmed, and friendly Indians have come many miles to inform the Mormons that poles were down in some solitude they crossed. They have not dared to touch the magic cordage themselves.

The Navajoes would give their wits to know the mystery of the "medicine" which frustrates their best-laid plans, and posts Bishop Winsor and his "merry men" on guard at the Pass, ready any hour to intercept the horses they may have stolen two hundred miles away! They have been foiled so often that, for the present, "the devil a monk would be."

One Indian of the Pah-vants rode for some miles beside the Beaver horsemen, leaning far forward on his saddle as he cantered along, his gay blanket dropped on the crupper like a riding-habit, his long, black hair and the fringes of his leggings fluttering in the wind of his going. But our horsemen soon dropped behind, waving courteous farewells to each carriage as it passed them. The road was rough; volcanic rocks cropping out and jarring us unexpectedly. The noonday halt was made at Buckhorn Springs, where we found but one little house, and at a short distance from it a stockaded enclosure for the animals. No garden, no trees, nothing but rock and sand to look at till our eyes rested on the mountains in the distance. The house stood on a slight elevation above the plain, and was inhabited by an aged pair who were wearing out the evening of their days in comfortless desolation. They had a fire burning on the wide hearth in their mud-and-log-walled cabin, and we went in to warm ourselves. The poor old wife's palsied head nodded so that we could not understand her; but a chance remark of T.'s regarding the brilliantly-colored woodcut of Beauregard and his Confederate generals that adorned the room, led the old man to overcome his repugnance to a Northern officer sufficiently to lead him to ask eager questions about Lee and Stonewall Jackson. Every answer that pleased him, he greeted like a primitive Methodist with a long-drawn "Ah!" or "Glory be to God!"

I listened to the wind which howled round the cabin as if it were a ship in a gale, while my husband good-humoredly gratified the old man's curiosity.

When we left the house the sun had dispersed the clouds, and the icy wind came from mountains bright with fresh-fallen snow. The sunshine was so brilliant, too, that the glare was unbearable, and the absence of coloring, except staring white and blue, increased the feeling I had of being at sea with a brisk north-wester blowing.

Hurrying into our carriages, we buried ourselves in the furs and prepared for an uninteresting afternoon. But we were not done with violent effects of color. There is no home-like scenery in Utah; a scene-painter's nightmare would be tame to nature's productions herewith rocks and sand. The afternoon was wearing on to the sunset when we came to a blood-red land, — cliffs, soil, and a crumbling old adobe fort, all red. Beside it a rushing stream dashed up wavelets of turbid red. Then came three or four red adobe houses, and some stacks of the brilliant straw-colored hay, with freshly-opened green hearts. The dreary wind howled and whistled among the walls and palings, and shook our carriages when we halted for a few minutes. Thankfulness overpowered me that, wherever else my lot in life might be cast, it was to be neither at Buckhorn Springs nor Red Creek Village!

Leaving the red cliffs behind, our carriages crawled through heavy sand at the base of a rocky wall which reminded me of Third Avenue, New York, as I remember it before the days of Central Park. It wanted only a street car, some stray bits of straw and newspaper, three Irish shanties, and a stencilled "Try Tarrant's Effervescing," to make me feel at home. The rendering of the wind-blown dust over the smoothly-slanting rock was perfect.

"Hark!" cried Evan, suddenly. "There's music. Listen!" We all laughed; for I had been saying this was like coming into New York, and Willie said, with the air of superiority which his nicer ear for music entitled him to assume over Evan, "It's only a cow mooing," and he pointed to a herd in the distance. But the gusts of wind soon brought the sound plainly. It was the brass band from Parowan come out to meet us, escorted by a troop of many youths. The horses danced and plunged as the band-wagon fell into line, and we entered Parowan in great state to the music of "John Brown's Body."

Our carriage. President Young's, and another drew up in the courtyard of Bishop Norman's low-roofed but wide-spreading home, and we stood a few minutes on the piazza to listen to the last strains of the band, and exult over the promise of a fair day on the morrow. Over the roofs of the town we could see that the snow-clouds were caught by the skirts, and trailing away over the mountains in the distance. The last rays of sunset streamed up a red and glorious background to the flag, which — forgive the scream of the eagle! — displayed its folds in the evening breeze from a liberty pole in the courthouse yard.

Parowan

Bishop Norman's comfortable house was one of those in which you feel at home at once. The very shepherd-dog on the piazza made friends with the children when they first stepped on the piazza, and "spoke" for a biscuit as if he had known them all his life. The master and mistress looked so like a Norfolkshire squire and dame, that I was surprised to learn that they were both from Massachusetts. Mrs. Norman was short, stout, merry, and dimpled: a suitable mate for Mr. Norman. She took me to my room, and when I rejoined her In the parlor introduced me to — Mrs. Norman. This one was tall, thin, serious and high-cheek-boned, and the two together reminded me of Hood's

"For I am short and she is tall,
And that's the short and long of it."

To repress my inclination to smile, I plunged into conversation, inquiring whether a young woman who appeared in the doorway for a moment, vanishing at a summons from the kitchen, was the tall wife's daughter. She replied, chidingly, "Certainly not!" and the plump one answered, merrily, "Oh, no. No, that's our Mr. Norman's third!"

Of Parowan itself, I saw little. The principal houses surround the courthouse square, and are shaded generously by double rows of cottonwood trees. These grow so fast that although planted only twenty-one years ago, in the infancy of the settlement, they give the town quite a middle-aged look, their branches already overarching the streets.

When we reached the end of a day's journey, after taking off our outer garments and washing off the dust, it was the custom of our party to assemble before the fire in the sitting-room, and the leading "brothers and sisters" of the settlement would come in to pay their respects. The front door generally opened directly from the piazza into the parlor, and was always on the latch, and the circle round the fire varied constantly as the neighbors dropped in or went away. At these informal audiences, reports, complaints, and petitions were made; and I think I gathered more of the actual working of Mormonism by listening to them than from any other source. They talked away to Brigham Young about every conceivable matter, from the fluxing of an ore to the advantages of a Navajo bit, and expected him to remember every child in every cotter's family. And he really seemed to do so, and to be at home, and be rightfully deemed infallible on every subject. I think he must make fewer mistakes than most popes, from his being in such constant intercourse with his people. I noticed that he never seemed uninterested, but gave an unforced attention to the person addressing him, which suggested a mind free from care. I used to fancy that he wasted a great deal of power in this way; but I soon saw that he was accumulating it. Power, I mean, at least as the driving-wheel of his people's industry.

Among the callers who dropped in at Parowan, my attention was drawn to a tiny old woman, who seemed blown into the room with a gust of wind, which was indeed so strong that she could not latch the door again after entering. Elder Potteau sprang to her assistance, and, looking up to thank him, she cried, "Oh, you dear, blessed man! Don't you remember me?"

"Sister Ranforth," Mrs. Norman good-naturedly hinted in a stage-whisper, and the Elder greeted her by that name.

"Yes; here I am. Look at me, so strong and hearty!" (She looked like a withered leaf.) "Don't you remember in '57, at the meeting in St. Mary Axe, when the brethren were all saying I was too old and feeble to go out to join the saints, that I said I wanted to start if I died on the way, that the Lord might know I tried to obey his words, and go to the gathering-in of Zion? And you said, 'Sister, you shall go. I feel to promise you that you shall reach the saints and see your children's children, and peace upon Israel.' And I *have*," cried the old creature, with joyful tears; "I *have* seen my children's children, and it's not four weeks sin' I held my first great-

great-grandchild in these arms. I wasn't quite ready to depart before; but I am now, and especially since I have seen you again. The Lord bless you, Elder Potteau, for the good words you spoke that day!"

Some of the women took her into another room to rest, for she was quite exhausted by her emotion. Her life seemed to be fading away with her color before our eyes.

The saints who are more used to his presence take Brother Brigham's arrival at a village tranquilly, but. new-comers in Utah greet him much more deferentially than if he were the President of the United States. There was a bright-eyed woman at Parowan with snow-white hair who tried to kiss his hand, and went round to all the party shaking hands with both hands and patting us. She had only been in Utah three months, and had come out with a train of indigent, almost destitute, converts. When such persons arrive, the bishops of the different wards provide them with homes and work, and Bishop Norman had taken her to his own roof, because her absolute deafness made her an unacceptable inmate to most people.

"But *I* can make you hear, can't I?" screamed the jolly wife into her ear, growing purple with the exertion.

The deaf woman nodded with a pleased look, as she replied, "Never once yet," Fortunately for Mrs. Norman's confusion, she went on to tell me that "never once yet" had she regretted leaving England. The saints were so good to her, notwithstanding her infirmity. I thought Mrs. Norman certainly was, when I saw how much trouble she had to make the sufferer understand anything. Mrs. Norman said she always went to meeting, and seemed to enjoy it as much as if she knew what was said there; and I noticed that one of the wives remained at home to take care of the house that evening to let Priscilla go to meeting, "because it was one of the few pleasures she seemed to have." She had been aged by a domestic tragedy, which whitened her hair in early youth, but her deafness had come on gradually.

She was a "servant" in the Normans' house, but, in the southern Mormon settlements at least, there is no distinction made between mistress and servant. The younger "sisters" think it no degradation to go to live in the houses of the married ones and help them with their work, and when work is over, they sit down to meals or "go to parties" together. I am not speaking of the rougher sort alone. I have met a wealthy bishop's daughter at a dance, dressed in white muslin, who has opened the door for me next morning with arms fresh from the wash-tub, when I went to call upon her mistress. It did me no harm when she shook hands on leaving me in the parlor, apologizing for being unable to remain with me.

Such girls sometimes marry their masters. A nice possibility for the wife hiring "help" to keep before her eyes! I met one woman who had claimed from her *mistress* the fulfillment of a jesting promise, — that if she served her faithfully for seven years, she would give her to her husband to wife. At the end of the seven years, she jilted a man to whom she was affianced, recalled the forgotten promise to her mistress's mind, and became her master's plural wife. There was no question of affection on either side. I believe she merely wished to share in his glory in heaven, with a modest competence here below. I give her up to you, father, to abuse to your heart's content. Apparently, she angled for a rich man quite as much as if she had not been a Saint. It is not for such as she that I ask your pity and sympathy. It is for those women who have become "plural wives" from a sense of duty, and who think their lot happy because they deem that God's blessing rests upon its hard conditions. I would have you pity Delia J., for instance, the wife of a man double her age. Of her the first wife said to me, "Delia is the blessing of my life. It is true that she has had trouble in polygamy. She could not bring her mind for a long time to see it to be her duty. But she is reconciled now. I thank the Lord every day that now that I am infirm. Brother Samuel has her at his side to watch over him, and see that his health and comfort are attended to as he is growing old."

Childless herself, this Delia is dearly loved by all the other wives' children, some of them older than she is. That first wife's eldest daughter said to me unaffectedly one day, when we happened to interrupt an earnest conference between her mother and Delia, Mother loves her better than any of us, and admits her into her inmost confidence; "because, of course, she is nearer to pa than we can be."

Pity her! I pitied Delia from the depths of my soul! I saw her wince once at an allusion to her childlessness, and thought how happy that devoted, affectionate nature might have made a home where she ruled sole mistress of the heart of a husband worthy of her.

Yet Delia was one of those who spoke most earnestly to me of polygamy as of divine institution, and rejected with horror the solution of the

Mormon difficulty which I advocated: that Congress should forbid any further polygamous marriages, but legalize those that already existed, seemed to me both just and merciful.

"Secure my social position!" she once repeated after me. "How can that satisfy me! I want to be assured of *my position in God's estimation*. If polygamy is the Lord's order, we must carry it out in spite of human laws and persecutions. If our marriages have been sins, Congress is no vicegerent of God; it cannot forgive sins, nor make what was wrong, right. 'Hard for me if polygamy were abolished, without some provision for women situated as I am!' Yes, but how much harder to bring myself to accept such a law as you speak of, and admit, as I should be admitting, that all I have sacrificed has not been for God's sake! I should feel as if I were agreeing to look upon my past life as a — as a worthless woman's — upon which I had never had His blessing. I'd rather die!"

How I detested her husband as she spoke! I felt sure *he* could not believe that that was a divine ordinance which sacrificed those women's lives to his. I heard him say that when "Joseph" first promulgated the Revelation of Polygamy he "felt that the grave was sweet! All that winter, whenever a funeral passed, — 'and it was a sickly season,' — I would stand and look after the hearse, and wish I was in that coffin! But that went over!"

I should think it had gone over! He has *had* more than half a dozen wives.

Parowan to Cedar

We had a serenade at Parowan as well as at Nephi, but I was so tired that I fell asleep before it was ended. T. praised the singing; and, in answer to my inquiries, told me that four babies, in arms, made their appearance with their mammas, the female singers of the choir.

Next morning, too, the brass band made their appearance as we took our departure; somewhat to the discomposure of the nerves of one of the horses, who broke away from the groom who was harnessing him, and after careering round the yard, leaped the fence, and galloped off to the open country. The time occupied in recapturing him enabled the band to give us a number of airs, and superbly well they played them.

Our morning drive to Cedar City was uninteresting; volcanic rocks, sage-brush, rabbit-bush, and grease-wood; on the plain the hills dotted with unpicturesque stunted cedars. Coming toward the city, we saw long fissures in the earth, five to ten feet across, and ten to fifteen feet deep, the result of drought. To compare large things with small, the plain was a grossly magnified representation of the undrained hollows on our country roads, where, after the puddles have dried up in summer, the clay is seamed with unpleasing cracks over which the yellow butterflies delight to sport.

Next we came to a ruined foundry, where the Mormons had made an attempt to flux the ores of the neighborhood. Much money has been made in Utah, but there are enough evidences of abandoned enterprises to show how faithfully the Mormons have endeavored to utilize the resources of the country and not dishonestly protect its manufactures. The best of the people wear homespun, and use inferior tools, and produce goods that return them but one per cent, on the capital invested, rather than look outside the promised land "for benefits the Lord has given them in it; if they could but exercise faith strongly enough to work with patience, and in spite of failure and disappointment, until mistakes are corrected by repeated experiments, and perseverance attains its end." Brigham Young is expected to put some of his capital into every good work, and this seems only fair. I believe that the foundry at Cedar City is to be reconstructed now that they have succeeded in finding a coal suitable for their purpose within easy reach; and I suppose that the Mormons' efforts to make silk, and cotton, and woolen goods, to work iron, produce sugar and molasses, wine, prunes, raisins and so forth, will finally be successful. They do not selfishly aim to put on the general market of the world an article which shall drive others out because it is the best and cheapest of its kind. Their ethics teach them simply to provide each settlement with some industry which shall make it self-supporting. The infant manufacture is expected to be encouraged by the saints, in spite of the temptations to purchase the cheaper Gentile productions that penetrate everywhere into the territory: in short, the manufacturers and consumers are expected to show their faith in Providence by flying in the face of Adam Smith. It would have been ludicrous, if it had not been pathetic, to hear the exhortations to saints who had been told off to Southern settlements where the desert had failed to blossom as the rose, and the torrid sun had disordered their livers. They were reminded that they looked upon their prospects with jaundiced eyes, and assured that it was only the weakness of their faith which made them fail to see the means of subsistence at their feet.

Had they tried the silkworm faithfully? There was Sister Murray in such a settlement who had done so, and succeeded. Had they tried making fuel of the tar of pitch-pine? had they examined practically all that might be made of the pitch-pine of the canons? Had they made mattresses of the fibre of the soap-plant, or dried it for exportation? I recall now a sanguine speaker running on with a dozen such bootless illustrations of the "capabilities" of the region in which we were, while I looked out from the open window of the meeting-house upon the barren, barren plain, which the poor saints of the congregation were vainly trying to improve. The plain sparkled in the sunshine. It was white for miles with soda! and the alkali was the most discouraging feature of the leprous landscape. But his hopeful disposition failed to suggest the idea that I hear is now under consideration at Washington. It is proposed that such lands shall be sold to future settlers at a higher price than ordinary government land; to wit, as if they contained coal and iron, silver or gold — in Washington English, as mineral lands. Had the preacher but thought of that!

Cedar City

When we fairly entered Cedar City I was pleased with its many long rows of trees. It is a (comparatively) old town, and they have had time to attain a very large size. The street where we halted was a shady avenue, and the lids drooped of my homesick Evan's eyes as the breeze rustled in the leafless branches arching overhead.

Under foot was a sheet of ice. The person whose duty it was to shut off the water at night that flowed through the streets, had forgotten to do so the night before, and the channels had frozen on the surface and overflowed and frozen again. We drew up before a large brick house in front of which a great bell swung. It had been made at the foundry, and when I suggested to our hostess that the noise it made must be deafening, so close to the parlor window, she answered with simplicity, "Oh, no; there's such a crack in it that it makes hardly any noise at all."

Our host was a blind man. Hardly yet in the prime of life, the terrible disease of the eyes which is so prevalent in Southern Utah had fallen upon him, and all the afflictions of Job, in the way of losses of cattle and other property, seemed to have followed. He would have been absolutely helpless, but for the exertions of his two brave little wives; little hens that scratched the barnyard faithfully for the support of the brood. They turned the house into an inn, and though it was but sparsely furnished, it was spotlessly clean, as I know; for I sat part of the afternoon in the kitchen. The wife who was busiest there had no children of her own, though one of the other wife's had been given to and reared by her; and she had the neat kitchen strangely furnished. One end was carpeted with oil-cloth, and in front of a window-full of scarlet geraniums stood a table with a brightly polished telegraph apparatus; and she turned from her stove and its pots and pans to her battery and clicking needle-point without flurry or embarrassment. I asked her whether it had not been hard for her to learn, for she was no longer young. She said "Yes;" that her fingers were inflexible, and that it had been very hard to eyes unused to delicate sewing and ears unpracticed to listen to fine differences of sound; but the Lord had helped her, knowing Mr. Hunt's need.

She spoke of herself as a rough and uneducated woman, though I found she had an accurate ear for music and a lovely voice in singing. But she had mastered her profession well enough to tell by ear what was going over the wires, and I believe that is considered a tolerable test. I like to see women telegraphing, it is dainty work well suited to our sex; and on our Eastern roads the officers tell me that the women telegraphers are more steadily attentive to their duties than men, and of course seldomer, I hope I may say never, stupefied with the fumes of tobacco or liquor. Their offices are cleaner, too, and gay with flowers, and those who for their sins are compelled to wait for a train at a wayside station often appreciate this difference. Still, women yield to one dissipation men are less apt to indulge in, and it was a characteristic that betrayed the sex of the telegrapher at the place we had left in the morning, when Mrs. Hunt remarked to her sister-wife that, evening that "Parowan has been called by St. George three times without answering. *She will go to meeting!*"

Mr. Hunt did what he could to help, poor fellow, and poked his way about with a long stick, as he directed his little boys in the barn and garden. They had a garden behind the house which must have been very pretty in summer, the large beds having neat box edges, and the main walk passing between fine peach trees.

His voice and manner, though melancholy and subdued, were those of a gentleman; and sitting apart beside the fire I overheard what was probably not intended for my ears. His little unkempt barefooted boys had followed him into the room. He sat down with my Evan on his knee, and passing his hand over the child's curling locks, and the fine cloth of his jacket, said to his own sons, —

"Lads, when I was your age I was dressed like this, and a servant waited upon me. When you grow to my age, remember I never grudged what I have undergone for my faith."

In the morning when we assembled for prayers, he was prayed for. Mormon-fashion, — "Bless his lids that the swelling thereof may diminish; and his eyeballs that the inflammation may cease; and the nerve of his eyes that its sensitiveness may be restored; and that he may see again the beauty and the glory of Thy Kingdom."

After we rose, as the custom was in many houses, the family sang a hymn; and it touched me to see him (although there were *two* wives which present repelled me), standing with his hand on the shoulder of one, the telegraph operator, while the other had her little ones grouped about her; and singing,

"Mercy, oh thou Son of David,
Thus blind Bartimeus prayed."

Poor man! His eyesight, I heard, did get a little better before we left Utah, and he became able to "see men as trees walking," and for even that cloudy vision he was thankful. As he said after prayers that day, "It might be the Lord's will to grant him sight, and if so his faith should not be wanting to enable him to lay hold of the blessing."

While I was acquainting myself with this simple household, T. was pestered in the parlor by some of the same class of mining speculators who beset him at Salt Lake City.

There were also plain farmers who had come to seek counsel of "Brother Brigham," whether to sell their farms to speculators, or to go shares with them in seeking minerals, or simply to plod on, using their coal only for family purposes. These gaped with open mouths at the glib, eager man, who had his pocket full of specimens from this and that neighboring mountain, and who pressed upon T. a share in his enterprise in return for a loan of the capital his worn boots showed his need of. These men had some really fine specimens, though their value was impaired to experienced eyes by their having been "doctored." Still, I do not mean to say that Cedar City has not a great future before it, possessing as it does, coal, lime, and iron ores in convenient proximity to each other. I hope Mr. Hunt's boys may share the prosperity of their birthplace!

T. presently made his escape to a more interesting group. Outside the windows near the big bell, stood all the winter afternoon a patient cluster of Indians. One sat on a rough pony, who stood motionless with drooping head, tired apparently by a long journey. The rider had his foot in a bloody bandage, and glanced from time to time at the parlor window. Did he hope the Great Medicine "Bigham" would come out and cure him? He never said anything, and rode quietly away at dusk. I knew "Bigham" couldn't cure him, but felt half-provoked that he didn't come out and make-believe to do so. The leader, a well-built, and, for a Ute, rather handsome man, could speak a few words of Mexican-Spanish. He bore a name common to many chiefs in Utah, but not then known to fame. He was a, but not *the* Captain John, Juan, or Jack. I transfer this mention of him from my note-book here, solely because I have a long story to tell of him, further on. He became possessed with the notion that he was divinely inspired, and did some frightfully queer things. I have seen something of insane persons, and a good deal more of religious enthusiasts; but a red Indian crazy upon religion, is the hardest character to understand I can conceive of. The belief of some of these characters in their most ridiculous fancies is absolute. One of them, for instance, who was recently an esteemed friend of this very John, ordered his followers to kill him, to prove how instantly he would receive a new body. He laid his head down: they chopped it off; and I visited his grave.

Kannarra

Our next stage from Cedar City was to Kannarra.

"Wrap up the children well," Mrs. Jane said, as we were about starting; "you will need all the warm clothing you have. We shall reach the rim of the basin this evening."

We thanked her afterwards for the timely warning.

Our way lay along a level plain, forming an avenue between mountains that gradually drew closer together toward the south, where opened the one wide pass of Kannarra.

Before sunset we caught sight of a great mountain ablaze with color, which we called Mt. Sinai. It stood apart on our left, half withdrawn behind two gray masses which we christened the Twin Friars: a natural rock portal revealing the entrance to a gloomy canon at their feet. Hard by, in the foreground, appeared some crumbling adobe walls, fast resolving themselves into the red earth from which they had sprung, and — emblem of desolation — an abandoned graveyard, where the gray tombstones were aslant, and half-buried in the drifting sand that had begun to wear them out of shape and efface the lettering of the names engraved upon them. The shrill wind was busy at its work of heaping up the sand on them, and blew a steady blast which penetrated all our mufflings. For the gorge we were passing was Kannarra Cañon, the true name of the great mountain was the peak of Kannarra, and the desolate ruins at hand were the abandoned village of Kannarra, from which the wind had driven the settlers. Absolutely nothing, not even a potato, they told us, could be grown there. The mere obstruction of a garden fence served to gather a mountain of sand when the wind rose; and one day the settlers were threatened with being buried alive, and the next, perhaps, a still stronger wind would sweep away sand, fences, roofs, and walls, and leave the plain smooth and naked as a sea-beach.

So they withdrew to a new "location," a little more sheltered, but still in the pass; for the Conference had decided it to be necessary to hold the post against Indian incursions. We reached this place shortly after. It was cheerless enough. Most of the houses were mere adobe huts; but there was one substantial brick building, and in this we were quartered. We had a spacious bedroom; but the skill of all the hospitable Roundhed family failed to induce the fire to do anything but fill the room with gusts of smoke; and we gave up, thinking that if the Roundheds could endure it all winter, we certainly might for one day. Moreover, as Mrs. Roundhed remarked philosophically, —

"It was a mercy it was *this* wind; because, if our stove drew, the fire in the sitting-room on the other side of the house would have smoked, and *all* the party had to sit there."

As it was, we were very comfortable beside the great fire that roared up the sitting-room chimney; and the children were amused by the draught that lifted the heavy cocoa-matting on the floor in waves. Whoever entered from outside came in with a surprising suddenness, and the door slammed to indecorously behind the indigenous visitor before he could get his breath to gasp out, "A welcome to Kannarra!"

Our hostess was almost bent double with sciatica, and appeared to be one of the saints who feel

"Earth is a desert drear, Heaven is my home."

Not that she did not set before us a bountiful meal, well cooked, and seasoned with hospitable words; but she seemed to think she had not yet found her abiding city, and that it was hardly worth while for her to set her affections on any place here below, — certainly not on Kannarra, Her husband's father had been one of the earliest of Joseph Smith's followers, and father and son had adhered to the faith with the tenacity of mastiffs. Every line of Roundhed's weather-beaten face showed courage and fidelity.

Those who are thoroughly trustworthy by nature may be sure that society will give their virtue full opportunity to develop itself. The unselfish, dutiful child in a family is always adequately "put upon." To the bravest soldier is ever given the honor of leading the forlorn hope. The Roundheds had been pioneers, I learned, in divers dismal settlements. They were among the founders of that "Happy Valley," in Nevada, where the dogs scratched savagely in the sand for places to cool their burning feet, and hens threw themselves on their backs and waved their claws in the air with the same end in view. I am not speaking in jest; I have the directest obtainable authority for the anecdote that Sister Morris found a young chicken on her parlor mantelpiece, which had hatched out from the egg there. It was one of three eggs, the first laid in the new settlement, set up on the mantelpiece as a special delicacy for her husband, and forgotten accidentally when "Colin cam' hame."

That sister gave up raising chickens, because the hot sand cooked the eggs nearly as fast as the hens laid them; and although the hens were willing to sit on them till they boiled themselves, nothing came of their devotion. This was in the charming Mormon "cotton settlement" on the Muddy River, called Saint Thomas.

Mrs. Roundhed, bent with sciatica, in windswept Kannarra, cherished tender thoughts of St. Thomas, where her rheumatism would certainly have been "thawed out."

I thought her situation unenviable, but the next time I came by Kannarra, when the snow lay a foot deep on her doorstep, I pitied her more. A month before, her husband had been detailed to head that exploring mission among the Indians near the San Francisco mountain, in Arizona, which caused so much speculation in our Eastern newspapers. She had been ever since shut up in in Kannarra, not knowing whether he was alive or destroyed by savages, or starved to death, or frozen down some half-mile-deep cañon of the awful Colorado. I had the pleasure of giving her the first news of his safety.

The messenger who had brought her husband word that he was set apart for this mission, told me that he arrived in the middle of the night. Mrs. Roundhed got up without a murmur, kindled a fire, and prepared a meal for him. As she watched her saucepan she heard the conversation imperfectly. She raised herself from her stooping position at the fire, and with one hand on her aching back, and the other suppressing a yawn, said, as quietly as if it were an everyday thing, "Well, Brother Gunn, I suppose this means another move for the saints? The Lord knows *I'm* ready!"

I am sure I hope she will be detailed to some settlement, on our own planet, where there are green pastures beside still waters.

Of course I saw Kannarra at its worst. Doubtless its winds are grateful in summer to those who toil up from the hot plains. And I am told that there is fine ranching ground only five or six miles off, fine coal, too, near and plentiful, and iron ore.

We spent Sunday at Kannarra. My husband and children went to the little meeting-house, whence the boys returned awed by their recollections of the hideous painted faces of some Pi-edes, who had flattened their noses against the window-panes of the building, back of where they sat. "Enough," Evy declared, "to give him nightmares for a year." As for me, I had found my first breath of keen air more than enough, and had withdrawn to the fireside, where I was entertained for the remainder of the day by one of the informal audiences I have spoken of

One brother was "breathing fire and slaughter" against the Pi-edes; and the bishop's exhortations having failed to inspire charity in his breast, he was brought to Brother Brigham to be "counselled" into submissiveness. I was told that he was a "rash man," venturing out alone from the settlements, and had been repeatedly chased by the Indians; and that "it was his brothers who got into the bad scrape."

"What scrape was that?" I inquired, desiring to hear some adventure with a triumphant end.

"Well, both his brothers and the wife of one of them were pursued and killed. They were not scalped; but they were stripped and their wagon robbed."

"By the Navajoes, I suppose?"

"Why, no," said my informant, sinking his voice, and looking cautiously at the bereaved brother; "they were Pi-edes; and unfortunately he thinks he recognizes one of his sister's earrings and a brooch of hers on one of them that are round here to-day."

It is hard to keep the younger brethren from avenging such wrongs promptly; but unless the case is clear to the criminal's tribe, punishment, however condign, would lead to a regular vendetta. But I really think the patience of the Mormons with the Indians surpasses anything we read of the Quakers or Moravians. You never hear the Mormon younkers boast of prowess at the savages' expense; their whole tone is different from ours. They talk, for instance, of the duty of avoiding *tempting* them by traveling alone or unarmed. The Mormon elders will not hear of vengeance on a tribe or band for acts committed by individual members of it. They think highly of the Indians' "sense of justice," and unless an outrage committed can be fully traced to some previous offense of a white, for which it is a reprisal, they obstinately attribute it to some "bad Indian," whom his chief would be quite as willing to punish as we would one of our white criminals.

Bishop Roundhed spoke of the bands of Navajoes of whom we had heard at Beaver. They had stated their case simply to him thus: If he would trade, they would be friends, and buy his horses with blankets; if not, as they wanted horses and must have them, he. Bishop Roundhed, could watch the ranches his best, and they would help themselves when and where they could. Said the bishop, "*I* had no horses, but I thought it best for the safety of the Co-op. herd to send up to the ranche for a lot of 'broncos.' They were some that we hadn't been able to do anything with."

Brigham Young nodded acquiescence, and I asked whether the Navajoes would buy unruly "broncos."

"Yes, indeed," the bishop answered, "and in a few hours they came riding back to Kannarra on the worst ones we had, as quiet as you please. The Navajoes are wonderful horse-tamers."

I asked whether their method was known. He replied, that they carried the horses out of the way to subdue them; but he had seen them rub a little of a red powder which they had with them, on a headstrong horse's nose, and bring it into instant subjection. They would not sell him any of this powder, nor tell him what it was.

Then Roundhed was bidden to propose a speculation to the next band of Navajoes that came alone. The "church herd" on one of the islands in the Salt Lake has multiplied fast, and there are now a large number of wild horses there. No one lives on the island, but a number of wolves dispute its supremacy with the horses; and the horses have battled with the wolves for life — the supplies of other food for the carnivora being scanty — until they have grown so fierce that no white man finds it pay to attempt taming them. The proposition to be made the Navajoes was, that they should tame the church herd on shares. They should receive one-half the horses for their pains: the Mormons to have first choice, however. Bishop Roundhed seemed to think the Navajoes would embrace the offer. He showed me seven fine blankets which he had received in exchange for one small mare. These Navajo blankets are said to be waterproof, and many of them are of beautifully varied colors; red, white, blue and black in the same blanket. Some are woven with complicated designs, evidently varying with the humor of the weaver. Unlike the lazy Pi-edes and Utes, there are Navajo men who think it not beneath their dignity to work, and will sit patiently on their heels in the sunshine all day twirling the spindle.

The different styles of Indian blanket vary more than our own do, but a connoisseur can tell the difference between a Moquis, an Apache, or a Navajo blanket at a glance.

I have spoken of the "Co-op. herd." In Utah they have carried the principle of co-operation very far, and finding how well it pays are pushing it in every direction. Each settlement has its herd, its dairy, its stores, its irrigating channels, and its fields managed on this basis; and the effort so far to restore the primitive Christian communism is entirely successful in settlements where the brethren live alone, without Gentiles to come in on them. One fence will enclose the harvest-fields or cotton-grounds of a whole settlement, each brother doing his share of the labor and being credited with his portion of the produce.

The excellent roads that carried us from one end of the territory to the other are not maintained at the cost of the entire population. The sums voted by the legislature are small, as the nominal taxation of Utah is very light; but the brethren from each settlement come out and make the road as part of the tithing of their labor. The bishops act as unpaid supervisors, and Brigham Young praises or blames each day's work as he comes to his journey's end over it.

Of course the tithing is not exacted from the Gentiles, and the Mormon roads are of great service to our miners for the carriage of their heavy freights. And, equally of course, the Mormons feel a little like the elder brother in the parable; seeing the prodigal's caravan rolling to the mines, where they cannot go.

Southern Ram of the Basin

We were told to prepare for eighteen miles of rough road when we left Kannarra, and we certainly encountered them. We were fairly in the rocks, and the lava blocks are the flintiest stones I ever heard ring against horse-shoe and wheel-tire.

The air was so clear that every object stood out in stereoscopic relief. The view was perpetually changing as our horses brought us abreast of openings in the gray mountain-wall on our left, revealing glimpses of a crowded world of red and yellow crags and peaks beyond. More golden sunshine seemed to rest on them than fell on us outside. For me to say that they were unnaturally vivid in color and harsh in their contrasts, would only signify that I was used to the gentle outlines and soft hues of Nature at home. Moses led his people forty years through such scenery as this.

Afterwards, we seemed to have come upon a great sloping down or moorland, sparsely studded with yuccas. Fairly tired out with gorgeous landscape and the constant use of epithetic adjectives, I had thrown myself back on the cushions, thinking, "Now for an uninteresting drive, I am glad of it," when the carriage ahead of us stopped and the driver came back to us.

"Brother Young says, 'Please watch yon crack, Mrs. T.'"

I lean out. There is nothing, surely, *there*. The sloping plain seems to have a fold or wrinkle in it, so that Its outline against the sky is broken, by a "fault," as our coal-miners would say — and resumes its slope, about fifteen feet lower.

For politeness' sake, however, I watch the "fault." As we approach, altering our course, I see that it is a crack in the earth, and that the road runs towards it. A few minutes more, and we are winding down a narrow road painfully excavated along the side of what I now see to be a chasm, sheer down which I can look hundreds of feet — and I much prefer not looking! But T. insists, and the children laugh at my cowardice, and I gaze in fascinated terror. We are so close to the edge that every now and then a stone our wheel has dislodged goes bounding down the precipice, hardly touching the steep side once before it strikes the frozen ice of the tiny stream below. We wind in and out of the corners of the great chasm, making short half-turns. President Young's coupé taking the lead. He stops when he has rounded each; and we see him looking out opposite us, almost within hand-shaking distance, it seems, until our more unwieldy carriage has safely turned the angle; and then as we pursue our way we see the remaining vehicles crawling along the curves we have just run. I am so glad to notice that one of the Mormon women is as great a coward as I am! She is burying her face in her hands, and her husband is rallying her as mine rallied me three minutes ago at the same spot.

We are descending rapidly. I find I like rounding the outer curve of the precipice even less than taking the Inner. The stream still falls more rapidly than the road, for I have made a hurried mental calculation that my courage can hold out until we have accomplished the five hundred feet of descent we first looked down upon. But we ought to have done that half a mile ago, and we seem to be looking down from a greater height still, "Oh me!" I exclaim; "is there no way of getting home In spring without coming back this way?" No, only this; unless I like to go down through the Apache country better.

At last we near the bottom. The stream, released from its icy fetters, dashes gayly at our feet, and we are level with the top of a magnificent stone-pine, the one and only big tree I have seen in Utah. No; here is another, sheltered by the great rock wall; and now we are out of Ash Creek Canon, and over the rim of the basin!

We had descended a thousand feet, the Mormons said. T. contradicted them; which I thought was a great shame.

The air was perceptibly warmer. A pool of water near which we passed was not in the least frost-bound.

The evening grew chill, however, before we reached Bellevue, a place which belies its name, being in a narrow valley between steep mountains.

There had been some discussion at Kannarra as to our remaining here for the night. Some of the party were in favor of pushing on, if possible, to St. George. Little Mabel had inspired my boys with an eager desire to stay at Bellevue, where she had spent a child's happy summer, and was positive that Mr. Dawes's barn could accommodate all the horses, and Mrs. Dawes's hospitality provide for all the travelers. The decision was to halt at Bellevue, and the female suffrage, I will not deny, was in favor of a late start next morning.

Bellevue

I had an impression that Mr. Dawes's farmhouse was a mere summer shelter for the family, to which they retired when the heat made their town house at St. George unbearable; and at best expected it to turn out an untenanted, barn-like place. I forgot that a Mormon could have as many housekeepers as he had houses. It was dark when we drew up at the kitchen door of the farm-house. A ruddy light streamed out, and our new hostess stood on the threshold to greet us. The kitchen was as neat as a parlor, and the aromatic scent of hot coffee came pleasantly to our hungry senses — the proof that we were expected. Another Mrs. Dawes, as trim, pretty, and youthful-looking as the one who received us, came from the stove, where she was superintending some delicate cookery, and the two conducted us to our rooms.

I had my choice of two equally comfortable ones, and found them both brightly carpeted, and well furnished. Summoned to supper, I entered a large, pleasant room, with a blazing fire, and a look of refinement about its arrangement that was in delightful contrast to the wild scenes I had been gazing on during the afternoon. In an instant Arabia Deserta had blossomed into Arabia Felix.

All our companions seemed in the best of spirits, and the mountains of rolls, the piled-up dishes of steaming potatoes, the steaks and chickens that our party made an end of before the more fanciful edibles, the cakes, and pies, and preserves were attacked, were enough to have justified the debate whether it was fair to come down on a Bellevue household on such short notice as we were compelled to give. But the little dames flitted about from parlor to kitchen, smilingly pressing fresh supplies upon us, and encouraging us to empty their great glass pitchers of delicious cream 'while we could,' as the milk at St. George was affected by the alkaline water and peculiar grasses.

After tea, the females, one and all, withdrew into the kitchen to "help wash up," — a performance that was enacted to the tune of merry laughter, and accomplished in an incredibly short time. A lovely little baby girl tottered into the parlor and signified her wish to be lifted on my knee, to the delight of my boys, with whom she began playing "bo-peep." The women then came back, and we talked around the fire till a late hour.

Outside I could see a light leaping up at the foot of the mountain, and was told that the telegrapher who accompanied us had tapped the wire and was taking down the news by the warm blaze. Again the anomaly: in this lonely place, in the mountain gorge, to hear read out, as I presently did, the news that would not be published in the great cities till the next morning, of what had taken place this day in Congress, and the latest European sensation.

This operator, a man of approved courage and strength of character, rode on a strong-limbed horse, never far from the President's carriage. He was so quiet and reticent that I did not discover his office, or that he had any, until we were half way on our journey.

The light of the telegrapher's fire drawing my attention to the window, I noticed that it, and all the others in the rooms I had seen, were shaded by long curtains of knitted lace. Mrs. Dawes had made them, she confessed with smiling pride. She had had plenty of time; for sister Fan. (the other little wife) had spent last summer with her, and, having been very sick. Fan. grew nervous, and liked her to spend the afternoon and evening sitting quietly by her bedside knitting. "'Fan.' did not live there, then?" "Oh, no; Fan. had a real nice house in St. George. She and Mr. Dawes had stopped for dinner on their way to a two-day meeting at Rockville, and the telegram came as they were sitting down. So, of course, they stayed to see us, and Fan, and she had been easily able to cook our supper between them."

This was a good-hearted little woman. Baby had evidently inherited her cordiality. My praise of her handiwork quite won her heart; and when I passed Bellevue on my way home, she had prepared a large tidy of the same lace, knitted from cotton grown at St. George, and spun at the Washington Factory near there, which she diffidently presented me with as a souvenir.

I often asked Mormon women — whenever, indeed, the question then before Congress was discussed, and that was very often — whether they would be satisfied if their present unions were legalized and all future ones prohibited. The telegraphic despatches of the evening having elicited a free conversation on the subject, I asked Mrs. Dawes's opinion. She was much embarrassed, being of a retiring disposition, and, I suppose, not a little afraid of an anti-polygamist questioner. She said she would rather not be asked. "Sister Dawes" (the eldest wife, a woman twice as big and twice as old, whom I afterwards met) "was a very good talker." (She was, indeed, a wonder in her way.) "But I," said she, "am very ignorant. And besides," she added, with a blush that dyed her cheek crimson, and a great effort to speak plainly, "it is not fair for you to take me as a sample of Mormon women, because I did not join the Church from conviction, but because my family — all my sisters — had embraced the faith, and were about leaving England. So I was baptized, thc last thing; and therefore, as for religion, I am not as strong in it as I ought to be. But I have married a polygamist, and have lived with his other wives cight years, and have been very happy. I took the position of Mr. Dawes's third wife; and I feel I should have no right to complain if he took another. But, then, perhaps, I don't know, never having tried being married your way. Sister Dwining, at St. George, where you are going to-morrow, — if you would ask her. She was married twice in the States before she joined."

At this there was a titter, I think, at the fair ingénue's expense, but perhaps my own!

At prayers that night I was struck by the unusual fervency of the petitions for the Lamanites (Indians), "that they might see visions and dream dreams that would lead them to embrace the truth."

I presume it was owing to a report two brothers from "Tocquer" brought of the doings of the prophet in the White Pine District.

To St. George

Going into Bellevue kitchen in the morning, I surprised President Young aiding our rheumatic Philadelphia D'Orsay to complete his costume. It was amusing to see John accepting every Civil Right "these yer Mormons" admitted him to as tributes to his monogamic superiority. Never a word of those profuse apologies which the natural politeness of colored people under ordinary circumstances would have prompted, on receiving such a courtesy from a white man seventy years ot age, passed his lips. He "stood severe in youthful beauty," and let the Mormon pontiff help him dress.

We left Bellevue under a cold gray cloud, in the shadow of the cliffs that overhung the valley. There was at first a gradual ascent to overcome. When it was surmounted, we found the sun was two hours high, and the view suddenly burst upon us of a vast field of mountain-tops, — a medley of shapes and colors. These were the last of the Wahsatch Rancre. We were coming down to the Rio Virgin and Great Colorado country, descending successive stages of levels, and changing the geological formation in which we were as we did so. After this, I was to see the supreme wonders of Arizona; but I could never again experience the bewildered admiration I felt that day. No one had prepared me for such a scene. The Mormons had kept it back as a surprise for T., who, when he passed up Utah from California, had come by the old Mormon Trail, by way of the Vegas de Sta. Clara, to Cedar City.

Far off in the east rose a chain of lofty mountains, their sides striped with party-colored bands, terrace on terrace, to what seemed a great city; its golden buildings crowning the summit. Behind its palaces the white towers of a cathedral appeared. The glowing colors were heightened by the snowy covering of still more distant peaks; some so remote as to be only faintly visible against the iridescent sky. The sun was now shining upon them in full splendor.

We halted to feast our eyes, and a geologically-disposed Mormon approached the carriage window to obscure our perceptions by explaining the spectacle scientifically.

"These rocks," he said, "are considered to be tertiary sedimentary strata; more or less horizontally disposed, with a tendency to cleave or split down vertically — hundreds of feet to a face. The strata uncovered are of different colors, red and rose-pink sandstones, gray and white-pink and tawny-yellow limestones and free-stones, and they are variously stained and striped by beds of ferriferous marl or marlite. They are also of different hardnesses, and weather down with varying degrees of rapidity. Fragmentary pieces of an upper layer of harder rock occasionally furnish water-proof roofs which protect the softer rock immediately beneath them. Elsewhere it wears down, and thus piers are left standing, fanciful pillars and similar resemblances. Hence arises the remarkable variety of pseudo-architectural scenery which regales your vision."

He ended with a concise little bow. I thanked him for his information, and took it down verbatim in his presence, but would have been better pleased to learn that I had looked at a Fata Morgana that was soon to fade away. There was something saddening in that distant view, of great courts and domes, empty and silent, with no human history or legend attached to them.

We were now, as I have said, over the rim of the basin, and rapidly descending; but still at a great elevation, with many summits to cross before reaching the plain. In all our turnings and windings, we saw from the top of each eminence this great group, "the Navajo Blanket series," as the children — bored with geology — termed it, still giving the distinctive tone to less marked ranges.

The foreground and middle distance were crowded with harsh contrasts to this rainbow beauty; the obliging geology of the region providing us with counterfeits of another style of human architecture, of anything but an urbane character. The ground over which we traveled was dislocated, disturbed on all sides by volcanic upheaval.

"Rocks on rocks confusedly hurled,
The remnants of ah earlier world."

Sometimes we crawled along the rim of an extinct volcano, the vast hollow of whose crater we had next to cross. Rounded blocks of lava, smooth and shining, strewed the fire-burnt sands, and our carriage was threatened with fracture at every turning of the wheel. Then we would begin to climb hills covered with similar blocks as closely as if they had been thrown at a storming-party in some Titanic fight in former days, from the gray fortress frowning at the top. My eyes assured me that the first one I saw was the work of human hands, until we had toiled upwards through the glazed stones for half an hour, and saw the walls assume their full size, and look down upon us as precipitous basaltic cliffs. The younger men of the party had all left the wagons, and hastened to help the horses, sometimes putting their shoulders to the wheel, sometimes blocking it with stones, when the exhausted animals paused for breath. At some turns in the narrow track, five or six would stand on the upper side of the road, and cling to each wagon as it passed, to keep it from toppling over. How frightened I was!

My geological friend reassured me, saying that we were almost at the top of the "mesa." The Spanish word was a novelty; and I fancied that it expressed the peculiar coping of the escarpment, until I remembered that it simply meant "table," and applied to the level above, which was supported by this fortress-wall. In a few minutes we had penetrated a gap, and were rolling smoothly along the sandy plain. Not all the carriages, however. A halloo from the men at the gap stopped us abruptly, as the last vehicle emerged on the summit, canted ludicrously to one side, its white canvas curtains flapping at every jolt like the wings of a great bird in distress. Poor Mrs. Jane's wagon was the wounded albatross. The jarring of the ascent had proved too much for it. While wheelwright straps and bandages were put on with Mormon ingenuity, — of course, precisely as prescribed by Brigham Young, — we alighted and walked ahead. Efforts were made to point out to me, in the dreamland under the horizon, the snowy peaks called Kolob. "Kolob" is the Mormons' "Land of Beulah." Somewhere, much nearer to us, but hidden by a black ridge, they said, was an isolated hill, known to the Indians as the Sacred Mountain. The Piedes tell that God and his saints came down in the days of their forefathers, more than a hundred years ago, and encamped on the summit, whence they descended to converse with men. To the disgust of the

Mormons, who liked the "Lamanite" legend, I hinted that this might be an indistinct tradition of the Spanish missions. Heroic Jesuits and Dominicans penetrated much farther north than this, centuries ago. The Sacred Mountain may have been one of their Stations. I have been informed that the names of several of them are recorded in Rome as having undergone martyrdom in these supernatural lands.

Poor fellows! Dream never constructed, in fevered brain, the image of a more hideous land to die in!

After this, anything like well-regulated landscape was lost in mere sensation. Everything grew red. The rock strata were of red sandstone: this was generally of a bright brick-red. The sands and earths, the result of their decomposition, over which we drove, were either a brick-red, or a shade more trying, which glowed, when seen under the sun's rays, a true flame-color. Once or twice, when this orange blazed against the black lava-blocks, we had the truly diabolic livery of our Lord Sathanas, —

"Blood and fire and vapor of smoke."

We experienced a sense of physical relief when we wound down from the last "mesa," and left "the Red Planet Mars" for our own placid green earth.

A black volcanic ledge shut out the last of the terrible grandeurs from us, and we found ourselves among flourishing settlements of human kind, chequered by squares of fields and regularly-planted trees.

We paused at a pretty little village, Harrisburg, I think, to water the horses at the stream which flowed through vineyards and peach orchards. A red mountain stood as a background, with a great arch in it which was conspicuous for many miles. Here it had been intended that we should dine; but we only watered the horses, and the two or three carriages that had come up rapidly followed us on. No lunch, and no stopping to feed the teams, and for the first time, no waiting for the slower carriages to keep up with us!

I wondered at it, and grew anxious, for several miles back my boys had begged to ride with Elder Potteau, and his wagon was out of sight. A little farther on we drove up a steep ascent and entered a dark cañon. There was a sudden halt — a little bustle. I looked out. By the president's carriage appeared half a dozen horsemen surrounding one whose horse's mouth was bloody, and who held a pistol in his hand. His own arms were grasped by two of the other horsemen, and his pale face wore a forced, fixed smile. I saw a man peeping at us from behind the rocks, who stole away unnoticed, and then the riders galloped off with the pale man among them.

What did it mean? I didn't know then; I don't know now; I often wonder. But, "placid earth!" Heigh ho!

Several other mounted men now appeared and cantered along beside our carriages; but we had no further adventures. My boys had been detained by another catastrophe to Mrs. Jane's unlucky wagon ahead of them, and did not reach St. George till late.

We now went on more soberly; if there had been any cause for alarm it was over.

For some time we had been noticing a change in the flora. At first a general tone of green was remarked; attributed then to the effect of the contrast in color of the rich, red soil; but afterwards not doubted. Sagebush and grease-wood gave way to cactuses like great shrubs, ilexes, acacias, and myrtles. By the time we reached the fields of Washington Factory, we saw green grass and water-cresses along the irrigating channels there. The carriage windows were let down, and we threw aside one wrapping after another, "marking how our garments were warm when He quieted the earth by the south wind." We were now fairly in the delicious climate with which our winter was to be blessed.

One more ascent, leaving the gray stone factory behind, with its cottonwoods fringing the dashing torrent, and we began the final descent to St. George, seeing the Rio Virgen sparkle in the distance under the last rays of sunset.

Twilight was falling, and the plain below us was in shadow as we came to the end of our journey. Smokes and trees softly intermingled in the evening air as we looked clown from the bluff upon the little town, and the gay voices of children playing reached us clearly. We descended, noticing a factory, a court-house, or town-hall, wide, red, sandy streets, trees with grapevines clinging to them on the sidewalks, pretty rows of small but comfortable-looking houses, each in its own vineyard among fig and peach trees. We stopped before a large house, where lights were already burning in our suite of rooms; and I uttered a cry of delight as I saw on the table the first letters from home! The dear, familiar handwritings were our welcome to Saint George on Christmas Eve.

www.ingramcontent.com/pod-product-compliance
Lightning Source LLC
LaVergne TN
LVHW050939080826
845145LV00004B/1323

* 9 7 8 1 7 8 9 8 7 5 2 9 4 *